GREYSTONE'S

Creative Hands

EDITOR

Beverley Hilton

GREYSTONE PRESS/NEW YORK · TORONTO · LONDON

Volume 2

Contents

Pattern Library

Embroidery appliqué

The silhouettes of antique cars make very good shapes for appliqué pictures. A framed set of three or four different models would make an ideal gift for a car enthusiast to hang in a den, bedroom or hallway. The one shown here has been cut out in large, simple shapes which are held in place with an outline of zigzag machine stitching. Details such as the spokes of the wheels and hand brake have been worked in varying widths of zigzag stitch. If you prefer to stitch by hand, use buttonhole and satin stitches to complete the design. Dress or upholstery fabrics make interesting textures, or you could use pieces of shiny plastic for some of the body parts, and metallic yarns for the spokes and metal parts. The background could be in a rough textured material, such as upholstery tweed, for an effective contrast.

Needlepoint 5

Make a lighter or glasses case

If you are not yet very experienced at needlepoint, you will find that both a lighter case and glasses case are quick, fun and easy to make. You can try out your favorite stitch to work all-over, rich-textured patterns, or you can use any of the other stitches shown here. Full directions are given for making both items, but you can give each one your own individual look with clever color and pattern combinations.

Stem stitch. Work from the bottom upward over 2 horizontal and 2 vertical threads. The spaces between the rows are filled with backstitches in a yarn of contrasting color.
Mosaic stitch. This is worked in diagonal rows from top left to bottom right of the canvas in groups of 3 stitches; over 1,2, and 1 threads of canvas.
Mosaic diamond stitch. This is worked in rows from left to right over 1, 3, 5, 3, and 1 threads of canvas.

Instructions for finishing needlepoint

Sometimes needlepoint, which takes quite a time to complete, can be ruined by nonprofessional finishing, so in order not to spoil your careful work follow these instructions.

Blocking or stretching
It is essential to allow for stretching purposes at least two inches of canvas all around the finished size of the work. The excess canvas is trimmed away to the required seam width after blocking. Needlepoint should never be pressed with an iron, as this flattens the textured stitches and ruins the appearance. Most stitches distort the canvas because of their diagonal pull and the best way to restore the canvas to its original shape is as follows:
Dampen the back of the work with cold water. Cover a drawing board, or old work table, with several sheets of white blotting paper. Place the work face down on the board and pin out, using drawing pins at one inch intervals. Pull the work gently into shape, adjusting the drawing pins. Dampen the work again thoroughly and leave for at least 24 hours, away from heat, until it is dry. When the work is completely dry, check for any missed stitches and fill them in.

How to make a seam

There are several seam methods suitable for needlepoint and this one is particularly good for small items which cannot be turned through to the right side after being seamed. The usual seam allowance is ⅝in, but for smaller items, such as a lighter case, ⅜in is sufficient. As canvas frays easily, it is a good idea to overcast the raw edges before finishing. With imaginative use of yarn and stitches, the seams can form a complementary and decorative feature to the piece of work.

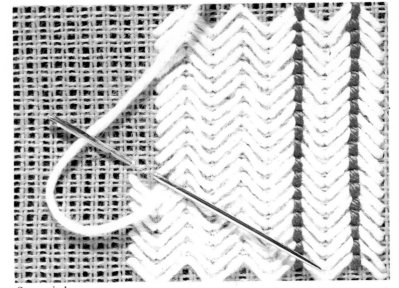

Stem stitch

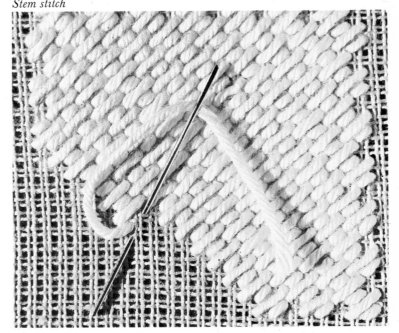

Mosaic stitch

Mosaic diamond stitch

Method

Trim needlepoint ready to seam and fold all seam allowances to wrong side of the work. Trim and smooth the corners and baste the seam allowance in place. Pin the two seam edges with the wrong sides together, matching up the pattern. Work whip stitch, cross-stitch or oblong cross-stitch along the seam on the right side, picking up opposite threads of the canvas from each side as you work. The seam when completed becomes part of the needlepoint.

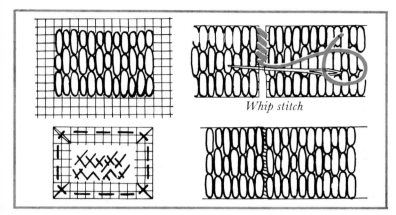

Whip stitch

Linings

The choice of lining is most important since it should not draw attention away from the stitching, either in color or texture. It is best to choose a firm, dull-surface fabric in a plain toning color. Pick the darkest tone used in the design because this will give strength to the design, whereas a light color will draw more attention to the lining than to the needlepoint itself. The lining seams can either be machine stitched or hand sewn with backstitch.

Glasses case

You will need: ☐ canvas ☐ yarn ☐ 4in length of cord ☐ lining.
Cut the canvas to measure 18½in x 6¾in, and cover an area which measures 14½in x 2¾in with stitches.
Block and trim the canvas, then cut a piece of lining material to the trimmed size.
To prepare the needlepoint for seaming, fold crosswise leaving a 2½in flap, wrong sides facing. Stitch the piece of cord securely to the seam allowance on the right side, one inch down from the opening. Baste edges and seam.
With the right sides of the lining together, turn up 6⅜in leaving a 2⅞in flap. Stitch the side seams from the fold to within ⅜in of the opening. Fold the seam allowance around the flap and across the opening to the wrong side of the lining, baste and press. Slip the lining into the case, using a blunt pencil to push it right down into the corners. Pin the lining around the edges of the opening and flap, matching the seams of the lining to the seams of the case, baste them together and slip stitch neatly into place. Remove the basting. Fold over the 2½in flap and tuck it under the cord, as shown in the diagram.

Lighter case

You will need: ☐ canvas ☐ yarn ☐ lining.
For an average size lighter case, cut the canvas to measure 6¾in x 10in and embroider an area measuring 2¾in x 6in. Block the canvas and prepare it for seaming. With the right side of the work facing you, fold it in half and sew the side seams, finishing as described for the glasses case, omitting the flap and cord.

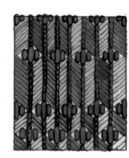

Lighter case

Lighter case

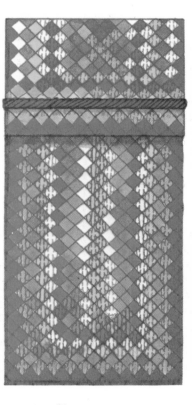

Glasses case

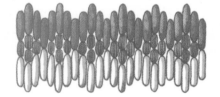

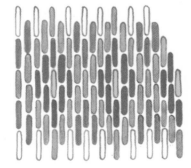

Some ideas for color and stitch combinations

113

Start building up borders

Once you've got the knack of making rows of needle-made lace, you can start building up all sorts of lacy borders, or you can use it to join two pieces of fabric with a decorative insertion. The lace edgings featured opposite are perfect for decorating handkerchiefs, small napkins, fine underclothes and delicate baby linen.

Trellises

Work from left to right. Make two rows of edging on the fabric, finishing at the left. At the beginning of the third row, start the first square by skipping two foundation knots:

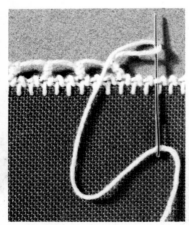

Insert the needle upwards through the next space, but before knotting it, measure out enough thread with the needle to form three sides of a small square (the fourth side is provided by the base). Tighten the knot and make three or four knots around the thread which forms the third side, ending with the needle facing upward. Continue forming the other squares in the same way, skipping two foundation knots and

114

measuring out the thread to obtain the two sides of the next square. Complete this row of foundation squares. Work from right to left and cover the foundation squares with a row

of knots, working about three knots for each square. Continue to the required length.

Loophole border

Build up basic edging to the depth required, then work solid sections alternating with loopholes as follows.
Work a section of knots in rows from left to right and back again until you reach the

depth you want. To make the loophole, skip 2 or 3 foundation knots and make a square with the thread as already explained for square trellises. Make a knot at the base of the square, then work a section of knots in rows from left to right and back again to match the first. At the end of each row on the square side, make the last knot around the thread which forms the third side of the square.
Over the top of the square,

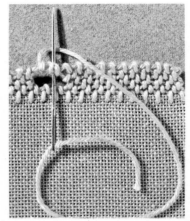

work the same number of knots as you skipped at the base.
Continue building the border to the required depth.

Simple lace

Hold the work downward, and work from left to right.

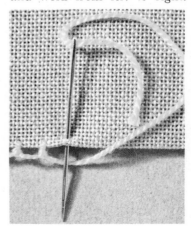

Inserting the needle downward through the fabric and passing it over the thread, make a small loop or blanket stitch. Finish the loop by securing it with a knot by passing the needle from left to right through the loop and tightening it firmly in place.

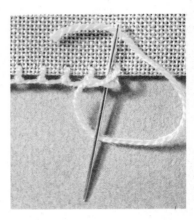

Double knot lace

Work from left to right, fastening off the thread at the end of each row. Insert the needle upward.
1st row. Pass the thread coming from the fabric over the needle to the right. Wind the thread from the eye of the needle twice around the point from right to left. Pull the needle

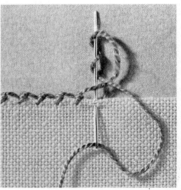

through, tightening the knot. Continue along the border, leaving about ¼in between each stitch.
2nd row. Work from left to right. Insert the needle through the first loop and wind thread twice around needle. Pull needle through, forming a knot.

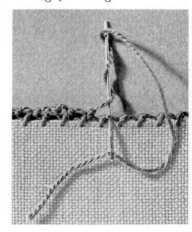

Lace arches

1st row. Work from left to right making knots as in ordinary needle-made lace, and leaving the thread loose between them to form small loops. If you find it difficult to

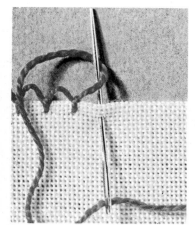

keep loops even, a pencil or knitting needle used as a gauge will help.

2nd row. Work from right to left in the same way, using the previous row of loops as a base.

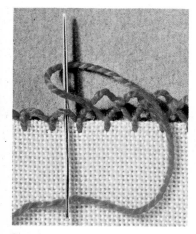

Bar lace

In this lace, bars are formed between the knots. Work the

rows from left to right, fastening off the thread at the end of each row.

1st row. Insert the needle upward. Make knots as for the first row of lace arches, leaving bars instead of loops.

2nd row. Make knots and bars from left to right by inserting the needle through the previous row of bars. Repeat these two movements.

Small buttonhole scallops

1st row. Work groups of four buttonhole stitches and loops.
2nd row. Work as for first row, working buttonhole stitches into the loops.

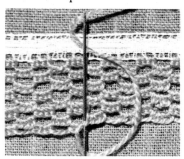

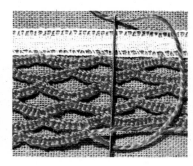

Large buttonhole scallops

1st row. Work a row of loops.
2nd row. Work over loops in buttonhole stitch.
3rd row. Work loops from the center of one loop to the center of the next.
4th row. Repeat second row. Repeat.

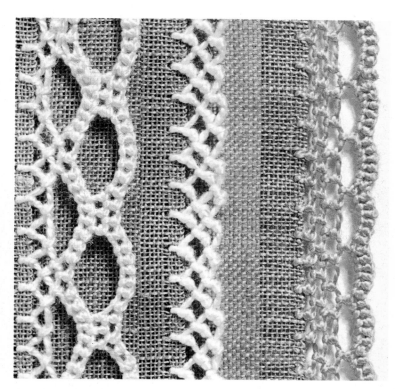

Lace edgings

The best thread to use is crochet cotton, because it is hard-wearing, it runs easily, is tightly twisted and gives the lace a consistent appearance. Be sure to keep the loops fairly flat or the edge may look ragged. The curves become pronounced as you work them.

Right border

Make three rows of bar lace. Work the fourth row with one looped stitch for every two. Work over each loop with six simple lace stitches.

Center border

Work three rows of double

knot lace (see facing page).

Left border

1st and 2nd row. Work as for lace arches.
3rd row. Working as for lace arches, * skip two arches of the previous row, make stitch into each of next two arches. Repeat from * across.
4th row. Work over loops with simple lace stitch, making 8 stitches in large loops, 1 stitch in small loops.
5th row. Make large lace arches, working 3 stitches in each large loop of previous row.
6th row. Work over loops with simple lace stitch, making 7 stitches in large loops, 1 stitch in each small loop.

When it comes to fitting-persevere!

Your skirt is now ready for fitting. It is a good idea to find someone to help you with this, because although it is possible to fit clothes on yourself, it is not always very easy to do if you have a difficult fitting problem, or, for instance, if you need to pin and make adjustments to the back section.

Slip on your skirt and pin together the opening for the zipper in the seamline. Adjust the skirt around your waist, lay the belting along the waist seam marking, and pin it to the top of the skirt.

Your skirt should fit closely to the figure around the waist and hips and fall to a gentle flare at the hem—it should not fit tightly at any point. Now comes the moment to get things absolutely right. The guide here shows some of the common faults, and on the next two pages you will find out in detail the best way to correct them.

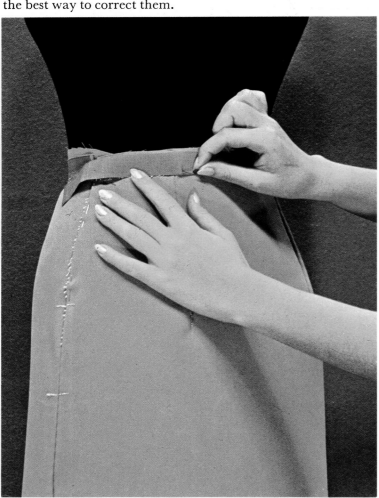

1. 'Pulling' lines across waist and hips
The skirt is too tight around the body.

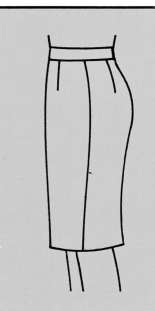

2. The skirt pulls in below the seat
The skirt is just too tight over the seat.

Fitting guide

Undo the skirt and pin new side seams all the way down.

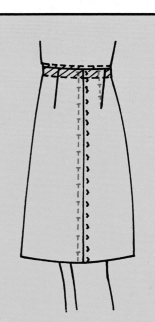

Pin new side seams on the back section.
Take any extra width at the waist into the back darts.

3. The skirt hangs loosely around the body
It is simply too big.

4. Creases below waistline at the front or back
At the back it's usually the combination of a long waist and a high seat.
At the front it's because your natural waistline tends to dip.

5. The skirt juts out at front or back hem
This means you have either a high stomach or a high seat.

6. Skirt juts out at front and back hem, and side seams hang inward
This usually means that your waist is large in proportion to your hips.

▲ *Faults and their causes ..... and how to correct them* ▼

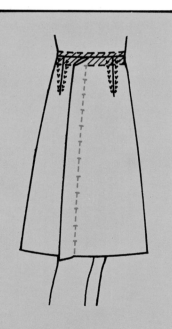

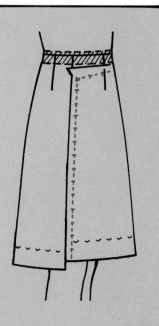

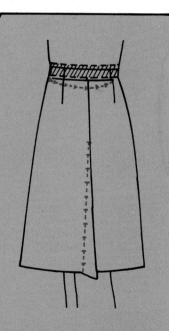

Pin away the fullness into the side seams. You may also have to let out the darts to allow the skirt to hang properly. If you do, take the extra material into the side seams.

The waistline requires re-shaping. Pin a crease across on the fabric below the waistband. Do not pull the excess up under the waistband as this will result in an incorrect waist fitting.

Pin a small crease toward the side seam on the section which juts out, enough to give you the correct hang.

Pin a crease below the waist-band and across the side seams so that the skirt hangs straight. Do, however, watch your hip-line as this may need to be taken in. If so, take in the amount on the side seam.

Tracing your alterations

Take your skirt off very carefully to avoid displacing the pins. Mark the alterations by tracing over the pins with long stitches in basting thread, taking care to catch in only one layer of material at a time. Trace the alterations on both sides, so that you do not lose all the markings when you take out the pins.

Remove the belting, marking any alteration you may have made to its length.

Marking and correcting after fitting

Now you are ready to correct and mark the skirt for stitching. The diagrams on the right show how to do this, taking each fitting in the same order as before.

Code:

- ☑ small checks = the original line of tailor's tacks
- ☐ red dashes = alteration lines
- ☐ scissors = where to trim off surplus material

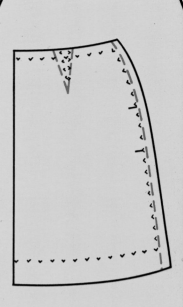
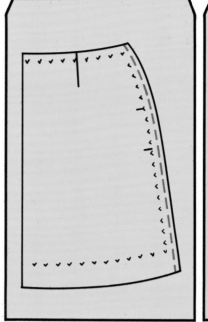

Fitting guide

Is one hip higher than the other?

If you have one hipbone higher than the other, first cover all the main faults mentioned in this chapter and then prepare the skirt for a final fitting.

You will then see how your high hipbone affects the general hang of the skirt. If it is not affected, you need only let out the seam slightly over the high hip in order to accommodate the higher curve.

If you find, however, that the hang of the skirt is affected, then you will need to adjust it on the opposite seam as well, by lifting into the waistband.

Transferring alterations to paper pattern

Once you have marked and corrected the skirt, it's a good idea to transfer the fitting corrections to the paper pattern right away, so that when this pattern is used again you can be sure of a really good fit.

To do this, measure all the alterations and draw them on the pattern in pencil. You can cut out the alterations to the waistline curve after first having made sure you have marked the pattern accurately.

If the skirt was taken in, mark the alterations to the side seams in pencil against the side seam on the pattern. Do not cut this off, since the same skirt made in another fabric may fit you.

Just make a note of it so that when you re-cut, you can baste the skirt inside the side seam line.

If you had to let out the side seams, extend the paper pattern by attaching a strip of paper down the full length and draw the alteration onto it.

1. Letting out side seams on both sections

Undo these seams all the way down and fold the pieces on center lines, as they were after cutting.

Measure the difference between the original side seams and the alteration marks on both the left and right sides of each piece of the skirt. On each piece, add the difference together, halve it, and measure this figure out from the original side seams, using pins or chalk. This is very important. When pinning the skirt, you might have taken up unequal amounts. The skirt would then be unbalanced if made up to the pin marks. Make a new line of tailor's tacks. Remove original markings.

N.B. When pinning seamlines, remember it's a good idea to lay the work flat on a table and bend down to look into the pin line at table level. You will be able to see if even one pin is out of line.

2. Letting out side seams on back section

Work as for (**1.**), but on the back section only.

Next, the darts.

You have already trace basted the extra amount to be taken into the darts. Now lay the back skirt section flat, right side up, and measure the distance between the trace basting at the top of each dart. Add these figures and divide into four. Turning the skirt section wrong side up, pin this amount off from the darts, starting at the waistline. Take up the fullness by running into the original stitching line at the point of the dart.

Make tailor's tacks over the pins to form a new stitching line.

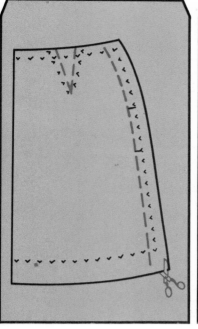
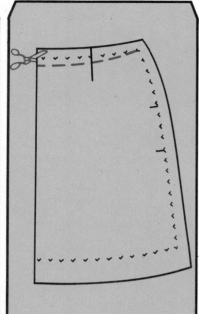
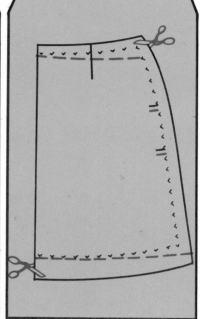
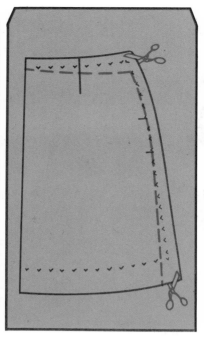

Take note ..... Take action

3. Taking in the side seams

Work as for (**1.**), but instead of measuring out from original side seams, measure in.

Let out the darts on the front and back sections in equal amounts. Pin off the surplus into the new side seams, starting at the waistline and tapering into the seam at hip level. Make tailor's tacks over this new line of pins. Mark the corrections with new lines of tailor's tacks and trim off surplus material, leaving correct seam allowance.

4. Re-shaping the skirt at the waistline

Turn the skirt inside out. Fold front and back sections on center lines. Pin the side seams together and pin along the waistline.

Measure along the depth of the crease between the trace basting and, starting with the full depth at center back or center front, pin a new waistline through the double layer, gradually curving up into original seamline so that the curve ends at the side seam.

Make a new line of tailor's tacks along the pin line and remove the original markings. Cut through tailor's tacks to separate layers and trim off any surplus material, leaving correct seam allowance.

5. Lifting a skirt that juts at the hem

Undo the side seams and to correct the jutting section displace the balance marks $\frac{1}{2}$in upward. The depth of the crease you pinned when fitting may not be quite correct, since the skirt was basted together at the side seams and you may need a greater displacement than $\frac{1}{2}$in. Try the skirt on again and check. Take care when you've reached the right amount of lift, as you may find it necessary to take in the side seam on the lifted section. Finally, level the waist and hemline. To do this, always level to the section which remains unaltered. In this way, if you lifted the front section, level this to the back section and vice-versa.

Make the new lines of tailor's tacks. Trim off surplus material, leaving correct seam allowance.

6. Lifting skirt at top of side seams

If it is necessary to take in the side seams, do this first. Undo side seams and lay skirt sections together, right sides facing. Measure the amount to be taken in. There will be more at the hem and less at the hip, with the line disappearing into the waist.

Use a yardstick to chalk out a straight line from hem to hips and then pin a gentle curve from waist to hips. Make a new line of tailor's tacks along pins for the side seams and trim off surplus material, leaving correct seam allowance. To re-shape waistline, pin and baste side seams together in new line, then fold skirt on center lines and pin side seam to side seam and darts to darts. Pin along waist seam.

Measure out depth of crease between trace basting and pin new line from side seam tapering into original waistline.

Make new lines of tailor's tacks. Trim off surplus material. Cut through tailor's tacks to separate layers.

Boudoir boots

Make these elegant indoor boots and soft shoe shuffle around the house in comfort throughout the winter.

You will need
☐ 1yd 36in wide fabric
☐ 1 pair of soft slipper soles
☐ 5yd $\frac{1}{2}$in seam tape
☐ Matching sewing thread
☐ 2 sheets of brown paper at least 12in by 16in
☐ Pencil
☐ Ruler
☐ Scissors

Suitable fabrics
Quilted nylon or cotton; upholstery fabric.

Making and altering the pattern
The pattern here is for shoe size $7\frac{1}{2}$.
Rule one sheet of paper into a grid of 1 inch squares. Copy the pattern and all details from the graph (figure 1) onto your grid, one square on the graph being equal to one square on the grid.
Cut out the pattern.
Measure the length of your foot by drawing carefully around it on the second sheet of brown paper. The length from the tip of the big toe to the heel corresponds to the straight line from A to B on the pattern.

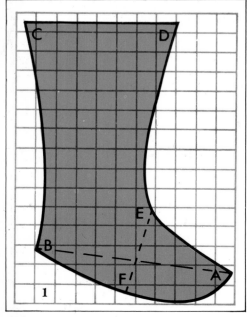

To make the pattern larger. Cut the pattern along line E to F. Lay the pattern onto the clean side of the brown paper and spread the two sections until line A to B is the correct length. Redraw the curves as shown in figure 2 and cut out the new pattern.

To make the pattern smaller. Cut the pattern along line E to F. Overlap the two pattern sections until line A to B is the correct length. Lay the pattern onto the brown paper (clean side), redraw the curves as shown in figure 3 and cut out the new pattern.

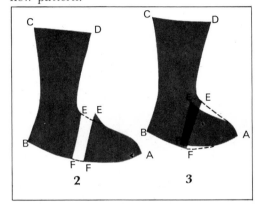

Making the boots
Cutting the fabric. Fold the yard of fabric in half, right sides facing. Pin the pattern to the top of the folded fabric and cut around the shape leaving a $\frac{1}{4}$ inch seam allowance. Unpin the pattern, and cut the other boot in the same way from the remaining fabric.

Joining the fabric. Place the fabric pieces together in pairs, right sides facing, and machine stitch from B to C and from D to A, with $\frac{1}{4}$ inch seam.
Machine stitch these seams again over the previous stitching to strengthen them.
Press the seams open and snip the seam allowances on the curves.
Cover each seam with tape and slipstitch the edges of the tape to the fabric, hiding the raw edges of the seams with the tape (figure 4).

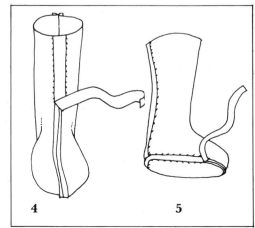

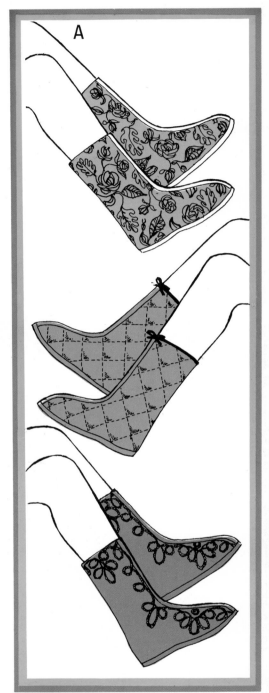

▲ *Choose a fabric to suit your mood*

Joining the fabric to the soles. Pin and baste the fabric to the soles matching the toes and heels and, as closely as possible, the edges. Using a fairly long stitch, carefully machine stitch the soles into place, with $\frac{1}{4}$ inch seams. Machine stitch the seams twice as before.
Open out the seam allowances, cover with tape and slip stitch the edges to the fabric and soles (figure 5).

Finishing the boots. Make the top edges of the boots neat by turning $\frac{1}{2}$ inch hems, covering the raw edges of the fabric with seam tape, and slip stitching into position. Turn the boots right side out.

Pattern Library

Needlepoint flowers

This charming stylized flower design lends itself well to being worked on fine canvas with pearl cotton No.5 for handbags; in tapestry or knitting yarns on coarser canvas for cushions, chairs or stools, or as a telephone book cover; and in rug wool on rug canvas for a carpet. So, take your pick!

The illustration includes a complete repeat of the design and is so clear that it doubles as a chart. Here it is shown in a mixture of violets, purples and raspberry colors on a sand background, but you could quite happily change it to morning-glory blues or whatever scheme you prefer. Work it in either cross-stitch, half cross-stitch or tent stitch.

Increasing step by step

Knitting can be straight or contoured, and it is by increasing and decreasing that we give garments the shape they need. Putting it simply, a piece of knitting is made wider by increasing the number of stitches in a row and made narrower by reducing the number of stitches. Interest is added in more ambitious designs by using these two processes to form patterns in lace knitting. In this chapter, step-by-step pictures show all the techniques from plain increasing to openwork lace effects. If you follow along and master these, you'll be just about ready to knit anything!

How to increase

The simplest way is to make an extra stitch at the beginning or the end of a row, depending on the shape you're making.
Do this by knitting or purling the stitch in the usual way, but do not slip it off the needle. Instead, place the point of the right-hand needle into the back of the stitch and knit or purl into the stitch again. Slip both these stitches onto your right-hand needle. You have now made two stitches out of one.

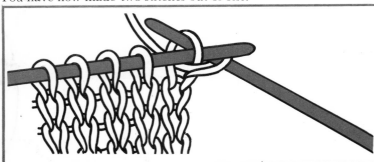

Invisible increasing
Insert the right-hand needle into the front of the stitch below that on the left-hand needle and knit a new stitch. If the increase is on purl work, then purl the new stitch. As it's almost invisible, this method is particularly good when the increase is not at the end of a row, or doesn't form part of a pattern.

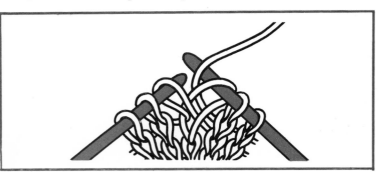

Increasing between stitches (M1K)
1. With right-hand needle, pick up the yarn which lies between the stitch just worked and the next stitch, and place it on the left-hand needle.
2. Knit into back of this loop. This twists and tightens the loop so that no hole is formed.
3. Slip the loop off the left-hand needle, thus making one stitch.

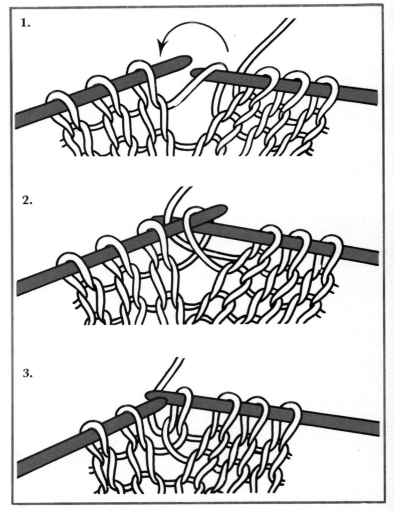

Increasing between stitches purlwise (M1P)
This is worked in the same way as for M1K, but the loop picked up is purled into from the back.

Multiple increasing
You will need this technique when you make a dolman sleeve. Cast on the required number of stitches at the beginning of the side edge, using the two needle method. At the end of the row, reverse the work and cast on.

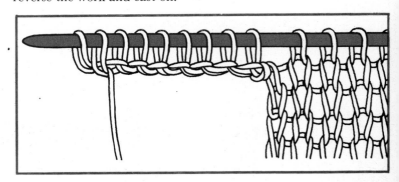

To make a stitch between two knit stitches
Bring the yarn forward (ytf) as if to purl, then back over the right-hand needle ready to knit the next stitch.

To make a stitch between a purl and a knit stitch
The yarn is already in position to the front, and the next stitch is knitted in the usual way, the yarn taken over the needle (yon).

To make a stitch between two purl stitches
Take the yarn over and around the needle (yrn).

To make a stitch between a knit and a purl stitch
Bring the yarn forward and once around the needle (yrn).

Decorative increasing

Increasing can be used not only to shape a garment, but also to be decorative at the same time. This way of increasing is usually made one or more stitches in from the edge, the number of edge stitches being determined by the pattern you are using or by your own preference. In the illustrations, three stitches are used for the edge.

The simplest lace effect may be obtained by lifting the yarn immediately after the edge stitches and then knitting into it. The end of the row is worked in the same way, lifting the yarn before the edge stitches.

A more openwork effect, shown in the illustrations, is made by knitting the edge stitches, knitting into the stitch below the next stitch on the left-hand needle, then increasing by knitting into the stitch immediately above.

To reverse this for the left-hand side of the work, knit to one stitch before the edge stitches. Knit the next stitch, increase by knitting into stitch immediately below this stitch, then knit edge stitches.

▼ *Increase at beginning of row*

▼ *Increase at end of row*

Crisp and carefree in crochet

If you've always assumed crochet was just for place mats or lacy edgings, then take a look at this eye-catching dress. It's crocheted in a firm, easy-to-do stitch. Look back to Crochet Know-how chapter 1, page 10, if you have forgotten any of the abbreviations.

Sizes

To fit 34 [36, 38, 40]in bust.
Length down center back, 35 [35, 35½, 35½]in.
Length of sleeve seam, 12in.
The figures in brackets [] refer to 36, 38 and 40in sizes respectively.

> **Gauge**
> 2 groups of 7sts = 2½in
> 24 rows = 5in

Materials shown here

3 ply Fingering Yarn
1-oz balls
8 [9, 10, 11] oz main shade, A
6 [7, 8, 9] oz in 1st contrast B
6 [7, 8, 9] oz in 2nd contrast, C
No. D crochet hook (or 3.00 mm.)
Two No. 2 knitting needles or Canadian No. 11

Back

With B, ch120 [120,134, 134].
1st row 1 sc into 2nd ch from hook, 1 sc into each of next 6ch, *yoh, insert hook into next ch, yoh and draw loop through ch, yoh, insert hook into same ch, yoh and draw through 2 loops, yoh and draw through all loops—this makes 1 knot stitch
124

(abbr. 1 kst), 1 kst into each of next 6ch, 1 sc into each of next 7ch, rep from * to end. Turn.
2nd row With B, ch 1, 1 sc into each of next 6sc, * 1 kst into each of next 7kst, 1 sc into each of next 7sc, rep from * to end. Turn.
3rd row As 2nd.
4th row With C, ch3, 1 kst into each of next 6sc, *1 sc into each of next 7kst, 1 kst into each of next 7sc, rep from * to end. Turn.
5th row With C, ch3, 1 kst into each of next 6kst, *1 sc into each of next 7sc, 1 kst into each of next 7kst, rep from * to end. Turn.
6th row As 5th.
7th row With A, ch 1, 1 sc into each of next 6kst, *1 kst into each of next 7sc, 1 sc into each of next 7kst, rep from * to end. Turn.
8th and 9th rows With A, as 2nd.
Continue throughout in this way working 3 rows alt in B, C and A, dec one st at each end of next and every 6th [8th, 6th, 8th] row until 91 [97, 105, 111] sts rem.
Continue on these sts until work measures 28in or required length to underarm.

Shape armholes

1st row Ss over 7sts, patt to last 7sts, turn.
Dec one st at each end of next and every 3rd row until 73 [75, 77, 79] sts rem.
Continue without shaping until 12 [12, 13, 13] color ridges or 36 [36, 39, 39] rows have been worked from beg of armhole shaping.
Fasten off.

Front

Work as for back until 8 [8, 9, 9] color ridges or 24 [24, 27, 27] rows have been worked from beg of armhole shaping.

Shape neck

1st row Patt over 26 [27, 27, 28] sts. Turn. Complete shoulder on these sts. Dec one st at neck edge on next 12 rows. Work 3 rows on 14 [15, 15, 16] sts.
Finish off.
Attach yarn to last 26 [27, 27, 28] sts, and work other shoulder in the same way.

Sleeves

With B, ch50.
Work in patt as given for back, inc one st at each end of the 10th [10th, 7th, 7th] row and every 3rd row until there are 77 [77, 81, 81] sts. Work until 18 color ridges or 54 rows have been worked.

Shape cap

1st row Ss over 7sts, patt to last 7sts. Turn.
Continue in patt, dec one st at each end of next 11 rows, then every 2nd row until 23 sts rem. Finish off.

Neckband

With No.2 needles and A, cast on 135 [135, 139, 139] sts. Beg with a P row, work 60 rows reversed stockinette stitch. Bind off.

Cuffs

With No.2 needles and A, cast on 68sts. Work 40 rows as for neckband. Bind off.

Finishing

Press each section under a damp cloth with a warm iron. Join side, shoulder and sleeve seams. Set in sleeves and seam the cuffs and neckband. Seam on wrong side around sleeves and neck. Fold neckband and cuffs in half to wrong side and slip stitch other edge to seam. Press all seams as before.

This versatile dress is just as good for a day in town as a country ramble ►

Covered rings

You don't need to be a crochet expert to be able to think up an enormous variety of exciting ideas for ways to use covered rings. All sorts of gifts and decorations rapidly take shape, and you will find that the materials for making them are very easily available and inexpensive.

You will need

Colored yarn. The ideas on this page were made using J. & P. Coats Knit-Cro-Sheen, but any not too thick crochet or knitting yarn would be equally suitable.

Rings. Select different sizes of metal or plastic curtain rings which you can get from hardware stores. You'll find this gives you greater variety than using only one size. A point worth mentioning is that with plastic rings you have the added advantage of being able to wash the finished article.

Crochet hooks. The size will depend on the yarn you choose. For J. & P. Coats Knit-Cro-Sheen, you'll need a No.7 steel crochet hook. For thicker yarns you need a hook which is less fine.

How to cover a ring

Insert hook through ring and draw a loop of yarn back through the ring. To secure end in place, pass both ends of yarn around hook and draw through the loop already on hook. This double yarn is used only for the first stitch. Continue working single crochet around the ring, keeping the stitches close together so that the ring is not visible. When the ring is covered, join the first stitch with a slip stitch. Cut yarn and finish off ends.

Card holders are useful

Cover a series of rings, as shown, and sew them together. Buy a length of wide grosgrain ribbon and sew the rings to the top. Make a loop behind the rings at the top of the ribbon for easy

hanging. This is a nice idea at any time of the year for displaying cards which you can't bear to part with.

Trim a package

A chain of rings joined together makes a gay and distinctive trim for any size package. It could also be an extra gift to be used as a belt, a hairband or, if the package is small, a bracelet. If it's going to be used as a belt, sew a hook and eye to the end rings on the wrong side, or attach cords for tying. For a hairband you can join the last rings by a small piece of elastic—when it's on the package, cover up the elastic with a bunch of gay ribbon!

▼ *Rings at the top of a card holder*

▼ *Rings trimming a package*

▼ *Covered rings forming a table mat*

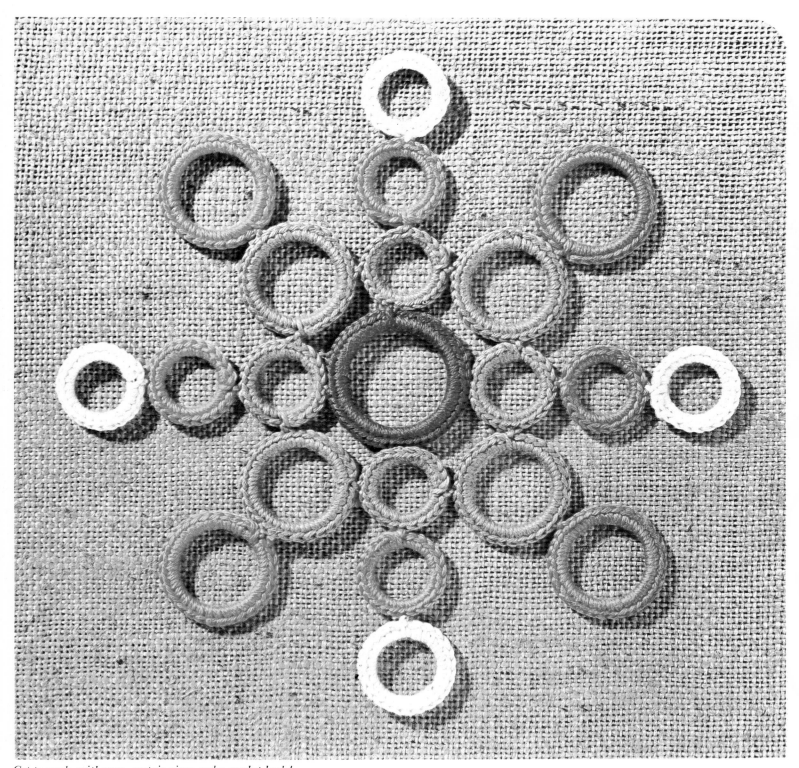

Get to work, with yarn, curtain rings and a crochet hook!

Make a table mat

Choose your own color scheme or combine the colors shown here. You can also have a lot of fun working out your own shapes using different sized rings. When you've covered them, here's what to do.

Lay the rings in place, right side down, on a flat surface. When they are in position, sew the rings together where they touch with a few small stitches, working from the center of the design outward, until the mat is complete. You can go on adding as many rings as you like to give variety to your designs.

Turning rings into buttons

Buttons are often difficult to find in the size and color you want, but you will never be at a loss for the perfectly matching button if you have learned to cover rings. This is the simplest button of all to make and looks attractive on knitted or crocheted garments. First, cover the rings. Then sew strands of the same yarn, like the spokes of a wheel, across the back of the covered ring. Using the same yarn, catch together the center of the strands and secure in place with a few small stitches. You can then use this center to sew the stitches through when you attach the button to the garment.

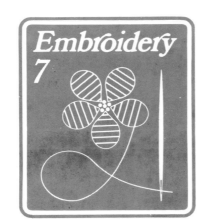

Filling in the outlines

Long and short stitch, split stitch and Romanian stitch are excellent filling stitches for feathery and furry textures. By introducing different tones of one color you can produce subtle and realistic shading for flowers, plants and animals. When you try out a new stitch, it's a good idea to practice on a small motif first to get the 'feel' of the stitch. Arrange one or two leaves or simple heart shapes on a place mat or tablecloth, or work the tiny Brimstone butterfly on a dressing gown or bedspread—and, if it's a particularly large bedspread, dot them around or work them in small groups.

Long and short stitch

Long and short stitch is worked very much like satin stitch, and takes its name from the irregular method of starting the first row of stitches. This stitch should be worked in a frame for the best results.

Start at the outline and make the first row of stitches alternately long and short, following the outline of the shape closely. Then fill in the rest of the shape with rows of stitches of the same length, fitting them into the spaces left by the row before, to give a smooth texture. The

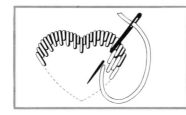

length of the stitch should only vary when you are filling in uneven shapes and you must be careful in grading the stitches for these shapes to produce a neat finish. For a smoother effect, use split stitch rather than long and short stitch.

Detail of butterfly shown through magnifying glass ▼

Romanian stitch

This filling stitch can be used in many ways to give different effects. As it is shown in the diagram, it is useful for filling in leaf or petal shapes. It can also be worked between two parallel lines, either straight or curved, with the stitches placed closely together. For shading, work each stitch with slight spaces in between, then work the next row of stitches into the spaces.

Bring the needle out at the left of the shape at A, take the needle across and make a stitch on the right side of the shape with the thread below the needle.

Make a stitch at the left side at B with the thread above the needle. Continue until the shape is filled. The center crossing stitch can be varied to make a longer slanting stitch or a small straight stitch for different fillings.

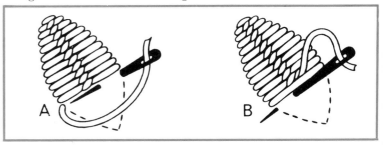

Split stitch

This stitch looks much like the chain stitch and is ideal for outlining. It can also be stitched in curving and spiral lines in close fillings as well as in straight lines.

Starting at A, make a stitch AB and bring the needle through again at C halfway along the stitch just made, splitting each thread into equal halves. The stitches can be gradually increased or decreased in length to fill the shape, but each should be brought up close to the center of the one before. When you are working curves use shorter stitches.

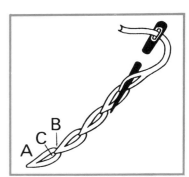

Leaf motif being worked in split stitch ▼

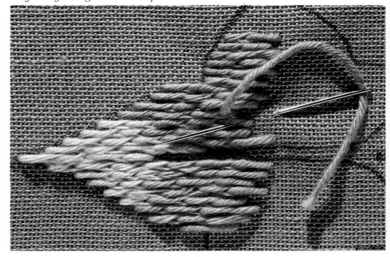

Dark outlines on head, tail
and feet.
3371

813
210

744

794
415

415

745

828

813

828

813
210

436   435
434   433

801

762
415

3371

762
415

744

Love a duck ?

This amiable duck shows how long and short stitch, when worked in a thread like pearl cotton, produces a lovely sleek feathery texture. See how soft and downy his breast is in contrast to the crisper, shiny effect of satin stitch on his tail feathers. These stitches are only suggestions. You might prefer to work the tail feathers and parts of the wings in Romanian stitch to add more texture, or, for quicker results, just embroider the details in line stitches.

It is important to consider the relation between the stitches you are using and the fabric background. A roughly textured linen is an ideal contrast to the smooth and shiny stitchery. This makes the duck stand out from the background.

On a smooth, shiny surface, it would blend in with the fabric and lose impact.
Trace the duck from the chart, and use it for your color scheme. All numbers in the chart refer to D.M.C. pearl cotton shades, size 8.

Collector's Piece

Chelsea carpet

Persia has always been famous for its beautiful carpets, and the craft reached its peak of perfection in technique, color and design during the 16th century. As scarcely any earlier carpets now exist, it is not known how long before that date Persia first produced them.

The Chelsea carpet illustrated here is a particularly fine example. It was discovered in an antique shop in the King's Road, London and bought by the Victoria and Albert Museum in 1890. The colors are subtly blended and generally rather subdued, with nine or ten colors usually included in each carpet—wine, turquoise, ivory and blue being predominant. These ancient carpets were finished with selvages and warp fringes at the ends. Usually they depict a flower garden and variations of vines, flowers and animals. The designs are balanced, though never regular, comprising corner pieces, panels, figures and a central medallion, with a sub-pattern from the tendrils and flowers.

Two kinds of knots are used. The Ghiordes knot is symmetrical from side to side,

130

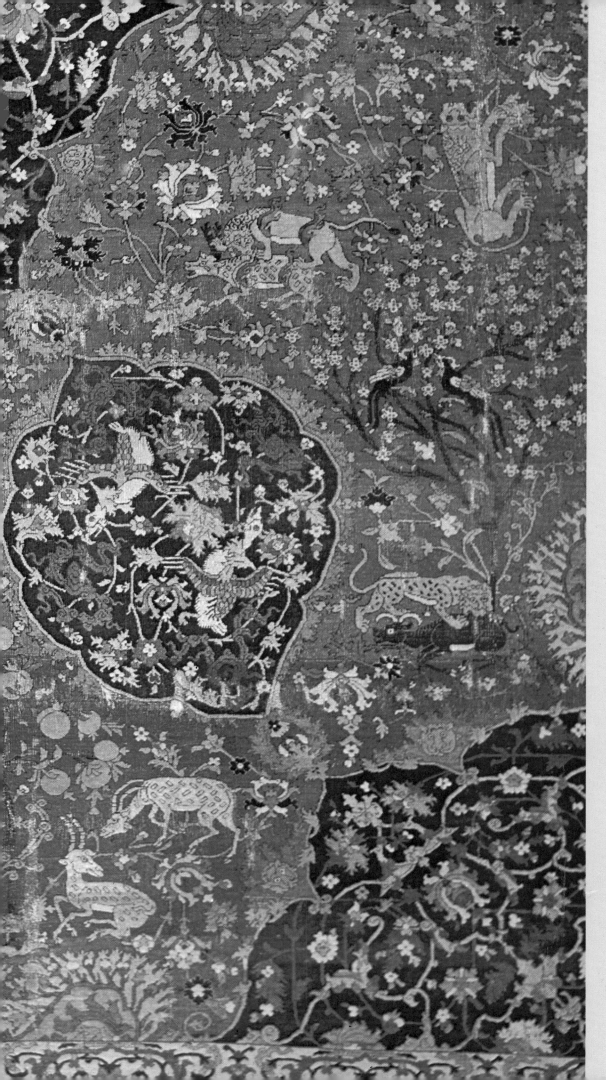

and is generally used for a one-level warp.

The Sehna knot is asymmetrical, and can therefore be tied as a left-hand or right-hand knot. (The right-hand knot is more common and makes the pile lie toward the left.) Sometimes, alternate warp threads are put toward the back to give two levels, and then the Sehna knot is tied around the front threads.

A fine texture is achieved by the Sehna knotting—the quality depending on the spacing of the warp threads (which may vary from 8 to 60 per inch) and the number of vertical knots. The quality also depends on the fineness of the yarn, and the number of plain rows of weft between each knotting.

More than 100 knots per square inch gives a fine texture. The Chelsea carpet, which measures 17.8 feet by 9.8 feet, has more than 45 knots per square inch.

The Ghiordes knot ▲

The Sehna knot ▼

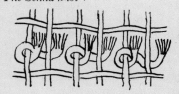

Latch onto rug making

When digging your toes into a cozy rug by the fire, have you ever longed to be able to make one for yourself? Well, here, with the help of Creative hands, you can learn how to do it. You will find all types of rugs in these chapters, from luxurious, thick-piled rugs and shaggy rya-type rugs made with a latchet hook, to delicate needle-made rugs with intricate oriental designs. Men have been known to enjoy rug making too, so see if you can get them to join in and help you, or let them experiment on their own.

Hooked rugs

Using cut wool with a latchet hook is one of the easiest and fastest ways of making a rug. The straightforward technique produces a warm, hard-wearing, thick pile that will last for a lifetime. There are three possible ways to go about making a pile rug. You can buy a kit with the design already printed on the canvas and the correct amounts of yarn in each color included; you can buy plain canvas with a charted design and choose your own color scheme; or, if you are adventurous, you can just buy a strip of canvas and make up a design of your own.

What you will need to design your own rug

Canvas: This comes in various widths from 14in to 45in, so there is plenty of choice for whatever size rug you make. A good size for a fireside or bedside rug is 6ft by 3ft. The canvas you need is 10 holes to 3in rug canvas and is usually divided up with either red or brown threads making squares, 3 inches by 3 inches, (10 holes by 10 holes).

Yarn: The correct yarn for hooked rugs is a coarse 6-ply rug yarn. This is available either in skeins, which can be cut to whatever length you want by winding the yarn around a grooved wooden gauge and then slicing along the groove with a sharp razor blade, or you can buy it pre-cut in bundles of over 300 pieces. These are called units and one unit will cover 3 squares with a little to spare. For the oversewn edge, buy skeins of yarn to match.

Tools: A latchet-hook is the only tool you will need and is available from any needlework shop. Shaped like a large crochet hook with a wooden handle, it has a hinged latchet which closes the open end of the hook as you make the rug knot, and prevents the canvas from becoming entangled.

How to start

Lay your canvas on a table with the full length stretching away from you. A good plan is to secure it with a heavy weight or a pile of books at the other end. Then, to prevent the cut ends from fraying, fold the end of the canvas over about two inches (raw edge uppermost), exactly matching each hole with the hole beneath. It makes the rug easier to work if you baste this in position. Now work the first few rows of knots through this double thickness, thus hiding the rough ends in the pile of the rug.

To make a really hard-wearing rug, finish it with an oversewing stitch around the edges. There are several methods for doing this (see Hooked Rugs chapter 3, page 172).

Leave the outside thread of canvas free and one square at each side next to the selvage so that they can be oversewn at the end. Start working the rug from left to right (right to left if you are left handed), and keep working in parallel rows. Don't be tempted to do patches of the pattern and then join them up, as this will give a very uneven finished appearance. Also, with thick wool it is easy to skip squares.

Ways to use rugs

Rugs don't just have to live on floors. In central Asia, for example, rugs are often used as decorative wall hangings. So if you have some bare wall space, try adding a colorful rug as an interesting new texture to the room. Or you could make a long narrow rug and hang it with big rings to make a cosy backing for a daybed.

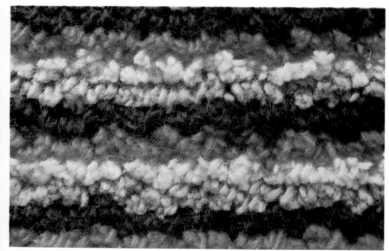

Two very simple but effective designs using combinations of colors in stripes

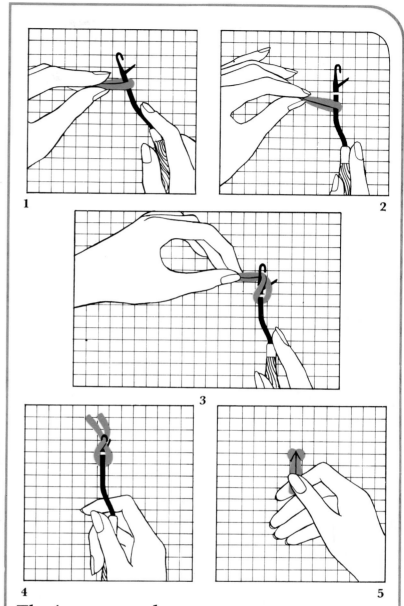

The 4 movement knot

There are two methods of making the knots in a hooked rug—the 4 movement method featured here is just quicker than the 5 movement method. (Directions for this are given in Hooked Rugs chapter 4, page 192.)

The difference between the two methods is the way the knots lie, which affects the direction of the pile. By using both methods, two people can work on a rug at the same time—one at each end—and when they finally meet in the middle, the pile will be lying in the same direction.

1. Fold cut length of yarn in half and, holding it between the thumb and index finger of the left hand, loop it around the neck of the latchet hook.

2. Still holding onto the ends of the yarn, insert the hook under the first of the horizontal (weft) threads.

3. Turning the hook a little to the right, take the ends of the yarn around the hook.

4. Pull the latchet hook under the weft thread and through the loop of yarn, catching the two ends in the hook as the latchet closes automatically.

5. Pull the ends of the yarn tight to check that the knot is firm. The tuft will end up lying toward you.

It's versatile, unusual and fun to do!

Make up-to-the-minute accessories using an ancient craft! Macramé differs from all other types of lace-making since all the knotting, braiding and tying is done by hand. You can use any thread from wrapping twine to crochet cotton, but make sure you use a strong, smooth twisted thread that won't unravel. You can either work macramé directly onto your fabric, or make individual projects based on a foundation thread. While working, be sure to keep the foundation thread taut. A good method is to stretch the thread across the back of a chair, or to fasten the thread with thumbtacks to a drawing board or the back of a sturdy picture frame—you can sit with the knotting board leaning against a table edge and resting in your lap.

Setting on threads

Fringing on fabrics

To work a fringe directly onto fabric, first calculate the length of the finished fringe desired, then measure the lengths of thread so that they are about eight times that length. Fold each thread in half (Figure 1),

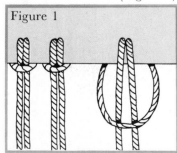

Figure 1

pull the double threads through the material with a crochet hook and loop them.

Macramé on its own

To work macramé separately, experiment first with a sampler before tackling a more complicated project.

Cut a length of cord to form the foundation thread, about six inches longer than the width of the planned macramé piece. Attach this thread horizontally to the working surface by tying the ends to each side of a chair, or by making a knot at each end of the thread and pinning these knots to a board to hold the foundation thread taut.

Calculate the length of the knotting threads—each thread should be about eight times longer than the length of the finished article. Heavy threads use up more length when knotted, so always allow for this.

Cut six lengths of yarn to the right measurement, fold each strand in half and tie the doubled strands onto the foundation thread. Do this by holding the doubled strand in front of the foundation thread (Figure 2),

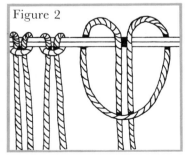

Figure 2

folding it over to the back and pulling the ends through the loop, tightening the knot.

Mount the knotting threads close together. When doing a large piece of work, you will find it easier to wind the surplus

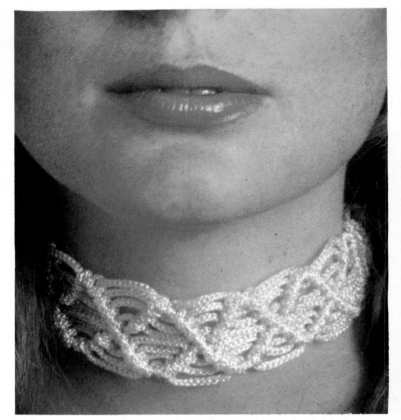

This simple choker is best made in a soft yarn with a shiny finish

thread into small bundles secured with elastic bands, from which you can feed out the thread as required.

Basic half hitch knot

Begin the macramé with a row of half hitches to give it a firm base. Do this by attaching either a second foundation thread at the top left-hand side of the work, immediately below the row of knots, or by using the left- or right-hand outside thread as a knot bearer. A separate thread should be six inches wider than the finished article. Hold the knot bearer taut in a horizontal position

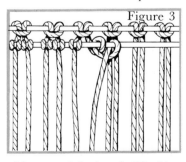

Figure 3

with your right hand. Working from left to right, bring each single knotting thread up in

turn, and wrap it around the knot bearer to form a knot. Repeat this process (Figure 3) to form a double knot, and pull each half hitch tightly into place before going on to the next. You will end up with twelve small half hitches.

Horizontal half hitches

As well as forming a firm base for beginning or finishing macramé, rows of horizontal half hitches can be used to vary a design. Horizontal half hitches are worked in the same way as basic half hitches, but using one of the end knotting threads as knot bearer, not a separate foundation thread.

Single diagonal half hitches

Half hitches can also be worked on the diagonal, sloping to the right or left. This is used to form a braid or diamond-patterned fabric. The left-hand outside knotting thread is used as a knot bearer (or leader) when working from left to right, and the right-hand outside knotting thread when working from right to left. Hold the leader thread diagonally downward to either right or left, depending on which way you are working. Take the second knotting thread and wind it twice around the leader to form a double knot (as in Figure 3). Continue along the row, knotting each thread around the leader until a diagonal bar is formed.

If when you've practiced making these knots you want to try something more adventurous, here is a simple choker to work in single diagonal half hitches.

To make the choker

You will need:

- ☐ 1 spool Cotton Glow Cord (1 spool contains 400 yards) or yarn of your choice
- ☐ 1 square inch Velcro
- ☐ Knotting board
- ☐ Pins, scissors, needle and matching thread

Cut six strands of yarn, each 104in long. Cut another length about 6in long, double it and pin it to the board to form a foundation thread. Double the lengths of cord and knot them onto the foundation thread.

Work two rows of horizontal half hitches as follows: Using the first knotting thread as a leader, work a row of half hitches across from left to right. Secure the leader thread at the right-hand side with a pin, turn the thread, and work another row of half hitches from right to left. (Do not use a separate foundation thread for these rows of horizontal half hitches, as the cord is usually bulky to sew in at the back.)

Using the outside thread on the right as a leader, now work a

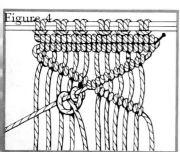
row of diagonal half hitches toward the center on five knotting threads. Using the outside

thread on the left as a leader (Figure 4), work half hitches diagonally from left to right across all eleven knotting threads. Take up the right-hand leader again, and complete the first diagonal bar from the center to the left.

Repeat this procedure until the length of the choker is the same as your neck measurement, then work as follows: On the next row of diagonal half hitches into the center, work from right to left over five knotting threads, and then from left to right over six threads. Now bring the outside threads down as leaders from the right and left, and work four rows of diagonal half hitches into the center alternately from right and left to make a pointed end.

To finish off

Turn back the threads and sew them down at the back of the work for about a quarter of an inch, then trim the ends closely. Do the same with the foundation threads.

Separate the piece of Velcro, and sew one half to each end of the choker, trimming the Velcro to fit.

Double diagonal half hitches

1. For double diagonal half hitches, use the left- and right-hand outside threads as knot bearers. Hold the left-hand outside thread diagonally downward, and make a basic half hitch over it with the next knotting thread. Continue along this row, knotting each thread twice, until you reach

the center.

2. The second knotting thread has now become the left-hand

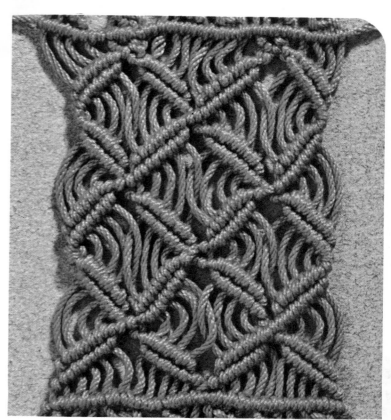

Here rows of diagonal half hitches create a diamond pattern

outside thread. Use this as the new knot bearer to make another row of half hitches below the first one and parallel to it.
3. Repeat this process, working from the right into the center,

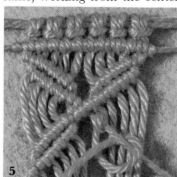

always using the outside threads as knot bearers.
4. Take both the second

leaders, which now meet in the center, and make a half hitch.
5. Working outward from the center to the left, make a row of half hitches, and then do the same, working from the center to the right. Return to Step **1**, and continue to the required length.

135

Give your skirt a neat finish

Having re-basted the seams and darts after alteration, and tried on your skirt again for a final check, you are now ready to stitch the darts and seams.

In this chapter you will find out how to put in the zipper properly, step-by-step, and how to stitch your darts for a really professional finish. Just to get you started, the illustration on the left shows you how your skirt should look when it is finished.

Seams and darts

Thread your machine with the same color as your skirt, and test the stitch length and tension on a double scrap of skirt material. It helps when stitching darts and seams to remember the shape of the human body. At no point where clothes cover us is there a sharp corner. Even the slimmest figures have gentle contours, so, when stitching the seams, always try to run the straight lines gradually into the curves. Switching direction suddenly will cause an unsightly pucker.

Stitch the darts and side seams, following the basting lines, and allow the dart ends to taper off smoothly. Start at the top of the side seams and stitch just outside the basting lines. If you stitch over the basting, it will be difficult to remove; also, as there is some 'give' in basting, your skirt might be too tight. Finish off the lines of stitching either by tying off the ends of thread, or by stitching backwards for about an inch to lock the threads.

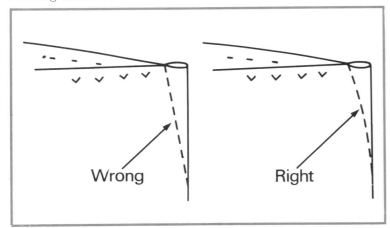

The wrong and right way to stitch a skirt dart

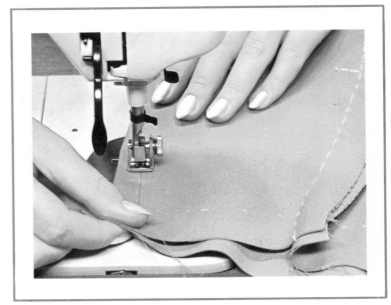

Stitching the darts

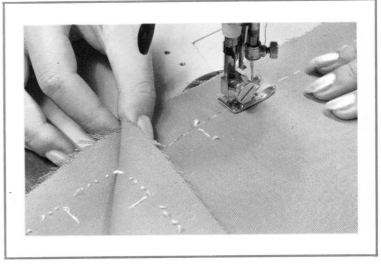

Stitching the side seams

Pressing hints

Pressing in dressmaking is quite different from ironing when it is just a question of smoothing out a surface. Pressing means fixing a certain shape which you have taken the trouble to fit and stitch. To retain this shape, use a lifting and pressing movement and adjust the pressure according to the weight and texture of the fabric. Some fabrics, such as woolens and linens, require a heavy pressure to stay in position—others, such as rayons, silks and man-made fibers need only light pressure.

If you use a damp cloth for steam pressing, do not keep the iron in the same place until the cloth is dry, but lift and press again repeatedly, until all the steam has gone. Even if you are working on fabric which does not need steam, it is a good precaution to use a dry cloth under the iron.

With some of the new man-made fiber fabrics, it is a good idea to ask for washing and pressing instructions when buying the fabric. As a general rule all fabrics made of man-made fibers should be pressed with a cool iron.

With mixtures of natural and man-made fibers, the seams may be difficult to press properly. In this case, use heat applicable to the base fabric, making sure at the same time that the fabric is protected by a cloth throughout the pressing.

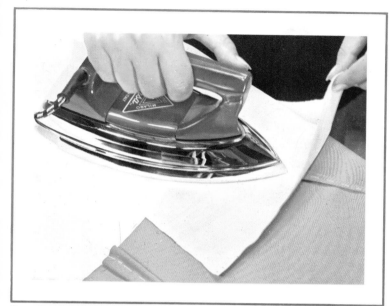

Pressing the darts

Pressing the darts and side seams

Some darts are turned to face the center of the garment and are pressed in that position—others are cut open to within 2in of the point and pressed open. But the darts on the flared skirt are pressed flat, with the center of the dart over the dart seam, which shows a neat flat finish from the outside.

Fold the dart centers to dart seams, pin and baste. Lay the pressing cloth (damp or dry, according to the fabric you are using) over the darts and press gently. Take out the basting and press again, to fix the shape.

Next, the side seams. Remove all basting other than the balance marks, lay the skirt over the ironing board and press the seams open, starting at the bottom. Do not press the side seams downward. The flare in the skirt means that the fabric is cut slightly on the cross toward the hem—and if you press into the seam starting from the top, you could stretch it.

When you have pressed the seam open and flat, you may find when you lift the edges that they have left impressions. Remove these by laying the damp cloth under the seam edges and, without touching the seam crease, press out the impressions.

Seam finishing

After the seams have been stitched and pressed, they must be finished off, to prevent fraying during wear.

There are various ways of doing this. If you are using a firmly woven fabric, use the zigzag stitch on your sewing machine to overcast the seams. Again run up the seam edges, not down, because, as with pressing, these edges could stretch if they are not stitched in the right direction. If you do not have a swing-needle machine, either overcast the raw edges by hand or just trim them neatly with pinking shears.

Putting in the zipper

First close the zipper opening with basting stitches and press open carefully, as for a seam. Take out all the basting and press again to remove any impressions made by the basting thread. As the seam is now open, take great care not to stretch the edges. Undo the zipper and, with the right side of the skirt facing you, lay the back seam edge of the skirt to the outer edge of the right-hand zipper teeth, and pin. When fitting a zipper, never stretch the seam over it, as this will cause it to wave. Also, the zipper and the seam should never be at equal tension; the zipper must always be held taut. If the opening turns out to be too short, undo the seam a little more to accommodate the zipper fully.

Pin across the seam to catch the zipper tape. After pinning, you should see the fabric rise a little over the tape between the pins. Baste the right-hand zipper tape securely into the back seam edge of the skirt with firm small stitches. Using the zipper foot on your machine, stitch the zipper in, about $\frac{1}{8}$in from the edge.

Close the zipper after stitching and lay the front seam edge to cover the teeth completely, far enough to meet the stitching line on the back seam edge. This will allow for recession when the zipper is stitched in, and yet still insure that the material covers it completely. Start pinning the front seam edge to the zipper from the bottom upwards, putting two or three pins across the seam edge and zipper tape. Then pin the top of the zipper to the seam, before pinning the rest. By doing this, you will easily be able to see how to distribute any fullness you might have had in the seam. If there is too much, ease this out toward the top. (It should never be more than $\frac{1}{4}$in.) Trim off after stitching, so that both top edges are level. Baste the zipper in firmly and machine stitch about $\frac{3}{8}$in from the seam edge. Then take out all the basting and press gently, wrong side up, using a cloth. This applies to metal zippers only. Nylon zippers need only the lightest touch when being pressed.

Overcasting by hand

Overcasting by machine

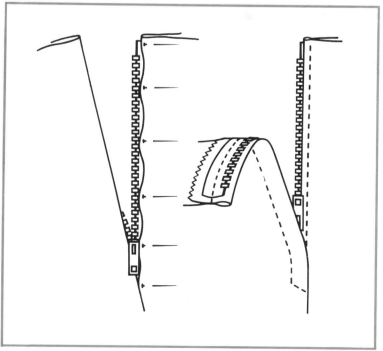

Skirt back seam edge pinned to the zipper   *Zipper stitched in position*

Making skirt hangers

For looped hangers cut two 6in lengths of straight seam binding to match the skirt. Fold double to form loops. With loops pointing downward, pin the ends ½in over the waist seamline, on the inside of the skirt, just behind the zipper on the back and 1½in from the right side seam on the front. Baste into position.

For flat stitched hangers cut two strips of silk or lining 4in long and 1in wide. Fold lengthwise and machine stitch ⅜in from the fold. Pull them through with a small safety pin and press flat. These are attached after the waistband is finished (see paragraph on waistband fastening on opposite page).

Putting on the waistband

Cutting out the waistband

Use the fabric from the bottom of the skirt length and fold it in half, selvages together.

Lay the waistband pattern on the fold and pin, first making sure that the fabric is lying perfectly flat. If you find, as a result of the fitting, you need to add to the length, now is the time to do it. Mark the waistband with tailor's tacks and cut it out, adding the same seam allowance as on the skirt, that is ¾in. Cut the tailor's tacks to separate the layers.

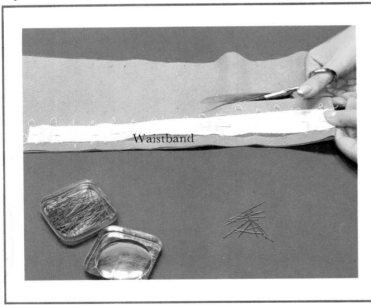

Cutting out the waistband

Stitching on the waistband

First measure the waist seam on the skirt and make a mark exactly halfway. This mark will be just in front of the right side seam, as all side seams in dressmaking are laid toward the back by 1in on either side. The length of the skirt waistline should be 1in more than the waistband. Mark the center of the waistband and pin into place on the skirt waist seam, matching center marks. Then lay the end of the waistband to the zipper opening in the seamline, back and front, making sure that the waistband is level with the seam edges at the opening.

The skirt waist seam is fuller than the closely fitting waistband because the skirt needs more ease immediately below the waistband to fit smoothly.

Distribute the fullness evenly between the center mark and both ends of the waistband, taking care not to make creases. Baste into position on the seamline. Remove all tailor's tacks. Stitch the waistband into place as close as possible to the basting line.

Mark the center of the belting, and lay it along the upper seam marks on the right side of the waistband. Baste firmly and stitch. The belting may be a little tighter than the fabric waistband. This happens through the natural spread of the fabric and will disappear when the stiffening has been turned under. Do not tighten the fabric waistband, as this could make the finished waistband buckle.

Remove all the basting, trim the waist seam on the skirt to ⅜in, as the double layer would be too thick, and press the seam into the waistband on the wrong side.

Turn under the seam edges on the front and back of the waistband even with the zipper opening.

Fold over the belting and pin.

Pin and baste the belting to the waist seam and sew by hand.

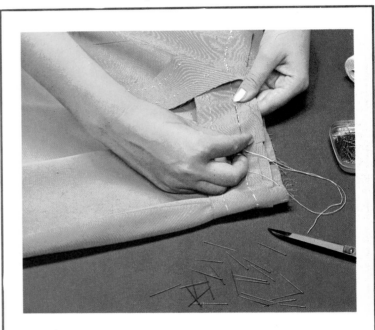

Basting the waistband into position

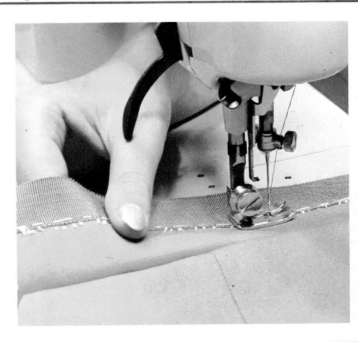

Stitching the belting to the waistband

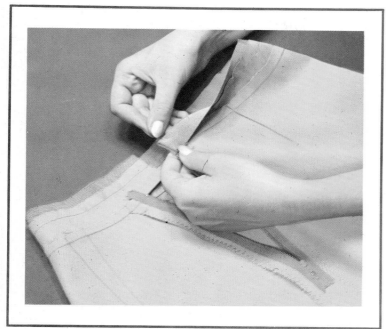

Folding over the belting and pinning

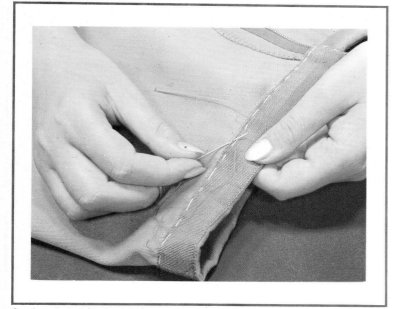

Sewing the belting by hand

Waistband fastening

Sew two hooks and eyes on the inside of the waistband, one at the top and the other just above the waist seam. Sew the eyes on the back edge, and hooks on the front. The loop of the eye should come over the edge $\frac{1}{16}$in. Hand sew over the sides of the loop and through each ring separately. Set the hooks back $\frac{3}{16}$in. Sew under the hook, over the double wire, and then through each ring separately. The hooks and eyes are sewn on in this way to prevent the skirt gaping when the give in the hand sewing makes them move toward each other slightly.

If you are using flat skirt hangers, now is the time to fit them lengthwise to the inside of the waistband. Do not loop them. Turn hangers under $\frac{1}{2}$in at each end, pin one on the back, just beyond the opening, and one on the front, beyond the halfway mark. To test their position, put the skirt on a clothes hanger. If the waistband droops, adjust the front skirt hanger until the waistband is level. Sew on securely by hand.

Turning up the hem

First pin up the hem along the line of tailor's tacks to check that the length is correct and that the hem is straight. If you have to level the hem or alter the length, ask someone to help you.

Before taking out the pins, trace along the crease of the corrected length with long basting stitches. Take out the old tailor's tacks. Before sewing the hem, make sure that the depth is even all around—measure this carefully and cut off any surplus.

Machine finish the edge with zigzag stitch, or overcast by hand, making sure you do not stretch the full sides.

Pin up the hem to the new line from the inside and baste about $\frac{1}{2}$in from fold edge. When pinning up a hem, always lay it on a table and insert pins toward the hem at right angles to it. This allows you to distribute any fullness evenly and prevents a twist on the finished hem.

Press the hem lightly with a cloth before sewing, remembering to press out the impressions left by the edge. Baste again about $\frac{1}{2}$in from the top edge, to hold the hem in place for hand sewing. Take the full depth of the hem into your hand and, without creasing it, turn under $\frac{1}{4}$in of the upper edge with your thumb. Sew invisibly behind the hem, taking up very little thread from the skirt and a good, deep thread from the hem.

Don't pull the stitches tight, as this will show through to the outside. Leave a little loop about every four or five stitches, which will ease itself into the other stitches. (This is a useful couture tip.) Always secure the ends of your stitches on the hem, never on the outside fabric.

Remove all the basting, and press the hem for the last time. Do not leave the skirt over an ironing board after pressing, as this would make little puckers on the outside of the hem. Lay it smoothly on a flat surface.

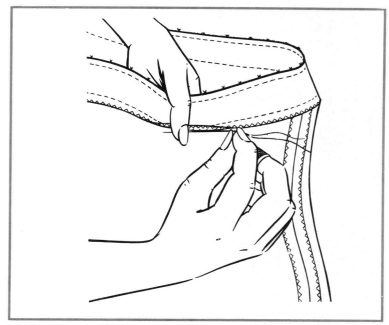

Hand sewing the skirt hem

Pressing for finishing

Pressing gives the final touch to any garment. Turn the skirt inside out and make sure you have removed all the basting stitches. Always use a cloth (damp or dry, depending on your fabric) and press the waistband firmly into place, still keeping the skirt flat. Then pull the skirt over the ironing board and press everywhere, except along the hem.

Fashion Flair

Ascot accent

Here you learn how to sew an ascot for yourself or the man in your life.

Suitable fabrics
Silk, shantung, fine wool, crêpe-de-chine, organdy and lawn (the last two should be starched for the best effect).

You will need
☐ ½yd 48in wide fabric or 1½yd 36in wide fabric (which will make two ascots)
☐ Basting thread and matching sewing thread
☐ Fine steel pins
☐ Sheet of brown paper 8in by 24in, pencil and ruler for pattern making

Making the pattern
Rule the sheet of brown paper into a grid of 1in squares. Copy the pattern and all markings from the graph (Figure 1) onto your grid, one square on the pattern being equal to one square on the grid. The pattern includes a ½in seam allowance.

Cutting out the fabric
Measure out and cut the fabric into two pieces, each 48in long and 9in wide.
Fold one fabric piece in half, right sides facing, and pin the pattern to the double fabric, placing it on the fold where marked. Mark points A, B, C, and D with tailor's tacks, through the pattern.
Cut out around the edge of the pattern. Unpin the pattern and repeat with the other piece of fabric.
Cut through the tailor's tacks. You will notice there are 8 markings for each letter A to D, arranged in two vertical lines of four.

Making the ascot
Place the two pieces of fabric together, right sides facing, and pin and baste around the edges, taking a ½in seam allowance. Machine stitch along the basted line, leaving a 6in opening on one of the long sides. Trim the seam allowance across the points and remove the basting.
Turn the ascot right side out and press carefully. Slip stitch the opening closed. Make two lines of basting to connect all the points A marked with tailor's tacks. Repeat with points B, C and D, making a total of eight parallel lines (Figure 2). Fold the ascot lengthwise, matching up the lines of basting between points A (Figure 3). Baste this fold into position. Match up and baste lines B, C and D in the same way, so that the center of the ascot is pleated (Figure 4).

Press carefully, only as far as the pleating extends. Make sure that the ascot edges are flat and that you press the pleats in the same direction.
Make four rows of machine stitching across the pleated section of the ascot at the points marked with tailor's tacks (Figure 4). Remove all basting threads.

His ascot
Make his ascot with a contrasting lining or embroider his monogram at one end. For the ascot with contrasting lining, simply cut one fabric piece from each color and make them up as before.
For the monogrammed ascot, mark the initial with basting on one piece of the fabric before you make up the ascot. Embroider the initial with stitches of your own choice, then make up the ascot as before.

Her ascot
Make your ascot delicately feminine or elegantly bold by adding decoration.
Sew a flight of lace butterflies around one end, taking the stitches firmly through both layers of the made-up ascot.
Sew a wide band of lace at a slant across the ascot. Hand sew each edge of the lace down through both layers of the made-up ascot.
Add your own initial in the same way as for his ascot.

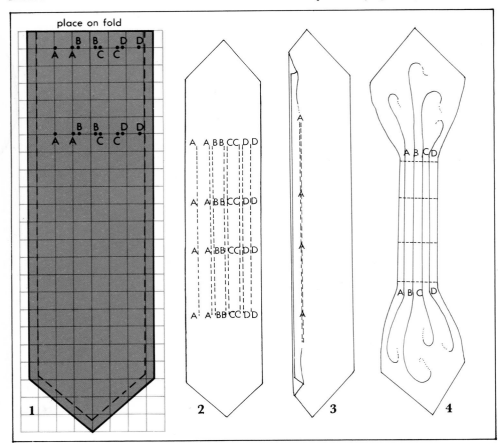

Pattern Library

Crochet flowers

Crochet flowers have almost unlimited uses. Appliqué several in a group on cushions or bedspreads, or add tiny flowers to frame a baby's bonnet. You can create an interesting effect by mixing yarns; for example, use a glitter yarn or fluffy angora in the center of a plain wool flower. With center color, ch4. Join into a circle by working a ss into first ch.

1st round. Ch1, work 15sc into circle. Ss to first ch.

2nd round. Join 1st contrast into top of last stitch with a ss, ch3, *skip 1sc, 1dc into next sc, ch1, rep from * 6 more times. Join with a ss into 2nd of 3ch.

3rd round. Ch1, into ch space work 1dc, 1tr, 1dc, 1sc to form a petal, *into next ch space work 1sc, 1dc, 1tr, 1dc, 1sc, rep from * until 8 petals have been worked. Join to first petal with a ss.

4th round. Join 2nd contrast with a ss between sc of last and first petal to begin 2nd row of petals, ch4, *1sc between sc at start of next petal, ch3, rep from * to end. Join with ss into 1st of 4ch.

5th round. Ch1, into first ch3 space work 1dc, 2tr, 1dc, 1sc, *into next ch3 space work 1 sc, 1dc, 2tr, 1dc, 1sc, rep from * until 8 petals have been worked. Join to first petal with a ss.

6th round. Join 1st contrast with a ss between sc of last and first petal of 2nd row of petals, ch5, *1sc between sc at start of next petal, ch4, rep from * to end of round. Join with ss into first ch.

7th round. Ch1, into first ch4 space work 1dc, 3tr, 1dc, 1sc, * into next ch space work 1sc, 1dc, 3tr, 1dc, 1sc, rep from * until 8 petals have been worked. Join to first petal with a ss.

Decreasing – simple & pretty

Knitting Know-how 8

Decreasing simply means shaping a piece of work to reduce the size, whether it is at the side edges of a garment or for darts, tucks or forming gussets. It can be worked so that it is almost invisible and may be hidden by seaming when you are finishing the garment. Also, decreasing can be decorative as well as practical. A good example of this is when it is used on the raglan shaping of a sweater or cardigan. If you work the decreasing on the end stitches, you will achieve a neat, hidden-shaping effect when seaming; or, if you try working the decreasing inside, say, two or three stitches, you will produce a fully-fashioned effect.

The way to make a simple decrease is by working two stitches together, either at the ends of the row or at any other given point.

To decrease one stitch knitwise (K2 tog)
Insert the right-hand needle point through two stitches instead of one, and knit together. This will slant to the right.

Knit two stitches together (K2 tog)

Purl two stitches together (P2 tog)

To decrease one stitch purlwise (P2 tog)
Insert right-hand needle point through two stitches, and purl together as if they were one stitch. This will slant to the left.
A simple decrease can also be made by knitting or purling through the back loops of the stitches and is then referred to as K2 tog tbl, or P2 tog tbl. This reverses the slant of the stitches.

To decrease using a slipped stitch (sl 1, K1, psso)
This method is most commonly used where decreases are paired, one slanting left and one slanting right as on a raglan sleeve. Slip the first stitch from left- to right-hand needle and knit the next stitch. With left-hand needle point, lift the slipped stitch over the knitted one and off the needle. This will slant to the left.
On a purl row the decrease, slanting to the right, is normally made by purling 2 together through back loop of the stitch (P2

Passing a slipped stitch over a knitted stitch (Sl 1, K1, psso)

tog tbl). You can also achieve the same effect by purling one stitch and returning it to the left-hand needle. With the right-hand needle point, lift the next stitch over and off the needle. Return the purled stitch to the right-hand needle.

Decreasing in pairs on alternate rows
When you are decreasing at both ends of a row and forming a line that will be seen in the finished garment, the lines should be paired so that they slant in opposite directions.
When decreasing on knit rows of stockinette stitch on the right-hand side of the work slip 1, knit 1, pass slip stitch over (sl 1, K1, psso). These stitches will slant to the left.
For the other end of the row use a knit 2 together (K2 tog) decrease. These stitches will slant to the right.
When used at opposite ends on alternate rows, they will then give you the inward sloping chain effect shown in the illustration.

▲ *Right hand side (Sl1, K1, psso)*　　　▼ *Left hand side (K2 tog)*

Lines formed by slanting decreases on alternative rows

Decreasing in pairs on every row

When decreasing on the purl side of the work as well as on the knit side, you should decrease in pairs to keep the slant correct. On the knit side use a slipped stitch at the beginning of the row and a knit 2 together (K2 tog) decrease at the end.

On the following row, use a purl 2 together (P2 tog) decrease at the beginning and purl 2 together through the back of the stitch (P2 tog tbl) at the end.

The alternative to purling 2 together through the back of the stitch (P2 tog tbl) is to purl the stitch and return it to the left-hand needle. With the right-hand needle point, lift the second stitch on the left-hand needle over the purled stitch. Return the purled stitch to the right-hand needle.

To make use of the chain effect, and to ensure that it is not lost in the seam when finishing, the decreases are often worked inside two or more edge stitches, the number of which can vary.

▲ *Purling 2 tog on purl side*   ▼ *Lifting st over st already purled*

Beginning to forget your abbreviations? Then look back to Knitting know-how chapter 1, page 7.

Twisted Decorative Decreasing

Sometimes the decorative use of decreasing is accentuated by twisting the stitches around the decrease to give them emphasis. This can also be given by incorporating a lace or eyelet effect into the decreasing.

The illustrations below show a decrease which is decoratively accentuated because it has been twisted and lies in the opposite direction to the line of the seam.

This decrease is worked at the end of right side or knit rows for the left-hand side, and at the end of the wrong side or purl rows for the right-hand side.

Knit to last 6 stitches, pass right-hand needle behind first stitch on left-hand needle and knit the next 2 stitches together through the backs of the loops, then knit the first stitch and slip both stitches off left-hand needle. Knit the last 3 stitches as usual.

On the next row purl to the last 6 stitches, pass right-hand needle across front of first stitch on left-hand needle and purl the next 2 stitches together, then purl the first stitch and slip both stitches off left-hand needle. Purl the last 3 stitches as usual.

▲ *Left hand side decorative decrease*   ▼ *Right hand side decorative decrease*

Gold & silver evening blouse

As a versatile addition to your evening wardrobe, try making this blouse that doubles as a lacy jacket. Wear it with your favorite skirt or over a plain sleeveless dress. Pick a thread with a lovely subtle sparkle—glowing gold, shimmering silver, gleaming bronze or lustrous copper. Combine two colors or use any one of them.

Sizes

Directions are for 34in bust. Length down center back, approx. 18¼ [19:19½]in. The figures given in brackets [] refer to the 36 and 38in sizes respectively.

Gauge

3¼ clusters to 1in
3 rows to 1¼in

Materials

Reynolds Feu d'Artifice, 20 gram balls
8 [8:9] balls in silver
6 [7:7] balls in gold
No. E crochet hook (3.50 mm.)
4 small crocheted buttons

Abbreviations

See Crochet Know-how 1

Back

Using the gold, ch102 [108:114].

1st row Work 3dc into 3rd ch from hook leaving last loop of each dc on hook (4 loops on hook), yoh, draw through all loops to form 1 cluster (abbrev. cl). Ch 1, skip 1 ch, *1 cl into next ch, ch 1, skip 1 ch, rep from * to end working 1 dc into last ch.

144

Turn.

2nd row Using the silver, join with ss, ch2, *1 cl into next ch sp, ch 1, rep from *, ending with 1 dc.
Leave the silver.
Continue working as for 2nd row, alt using gold and silver and working from the end where the required color has been left to avoid joining.
To start a new row, work a long loop and ss into edge of last row, work 2ch and continue in patt.
Work until 11 [11¼:11½]in from start.

Shape armholes

Keeping patt correct, work 4cl less at each end of next row, and 1 cl less at each end of following row.
Work without further shaping until armholes measure 6¼ [6½:6¾]in.

Shape shoulder

Work 4cl less at armhole edges and skip 1 ch after last cl, 1 dc into next ch sp. Turn.
Next row Work 3cl, skip 1 ch after last cl, 1 dc into next ch sp.
Break yarn.
Work other shoulder in same way.

Left front

Using the gold, ch44 [48:52].
Work in patt as given for back until work measures same to armhole.

Shape armhole

Work 4cl less at side edge.
Work without shaping until center front edge measures 14¼ [14½:14¾]in.

Shape neck

1st row Work 5cl less at center front, work to end. Turn.
2nd row Patt to last ch sp, skip 1 ch after last cl, 1 dc into edge. Turn.
3rd row Work cl into first ch sp, patt to end. Turn.
4th row as 2nd row.
Continue without further shaping until armhole measures same as back to shoulder.

Shape shoulder

Work as given for back shoulder.
Finish off.

Right front

Work in same way as for left front.

Sleeves

Using the gold, ch68 [70:72].
Work in patt for 6 [7:8] rows.

Shape cap

Work 3cl less at each end of next row.
Work 1 cl less at each end of next 13 [13:14] rows.
Break yarn and finish off.

Finishing

Sew shoulder and side seams.

Border

Using the silver, work sleeve borders.
1st row *1 sc into each of

next 4ch, dec in next 2ch by inserting hook into next ch, yoh and draw through ch, insert hook into next ch, yoh and draw through ch, yoh and draw through all loops, rep from * to end. Turn.
2nd row Ch2, *yoh, insert hook into next sc (yoh and draw through a long loop) 4 times in the same st, yoh and draw through all loops on hook to make 1 puff, ch 1, skip 1 ch, rep from * to end. Turn.
3rd row Ch2, 1 sc into the top of each puff and each ch to end of row. Turn.
4th row *Ch3, 1 dc into next sc, skip 1 sc, 1 sc into next sc, rep from * to end of row.

Finishing

Work other sleeve border in the same way.
Work border around jacket in same way starting at side seam and working 1 sc into each ch along lower edge, 1 sc, ch2, 1 sc into corner st, 2sc into each row up front edges, and dec twice on curves at front neck and once on either curve at back as given for sleeve. On the following row work 2ch between the puffs at the corners.
Sew sleeve seams and set in sleeves.
Sew on buttons if desired with the spaces between the puffs acting as buttonholes.

Detailed close-up of the pattern and edging of the gold and silver blouse

Cords, buttons, spirals and rosettes

Small crochet trims are easy to handle, quickly worked, perfect for using up all those left-over odds and ends, and are a marvelous way of adding finish and individuality to clothes and accessories. Take a baby's bonnet, trim it with bunches of cord and pastel rosettes like a miniature bouquet of flowers, and fasten mittens and bootees with ties trimmed to match. Add a bold military touch to a jacket with a richly scrolled frogged fastening and crocheted buttons. Dangle groups of crochet spirals from the ends of a slender cord belt. Make them in glittering yarn to fringe an evening bag, or let the whole idea go to your head with narrow cords or flower rosettes to twist into an elaborate party hair style.

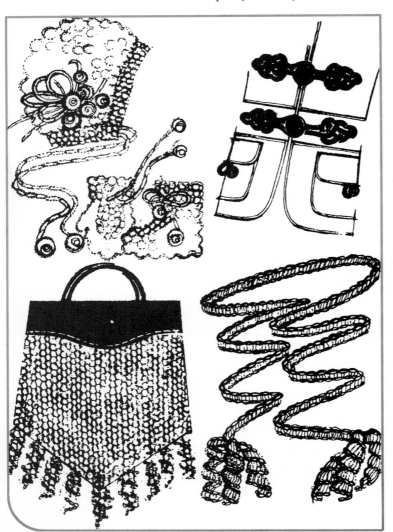

Cords

The cord on this page is made with double stitches, but single crochet, half doubles, or trebles would be just as effective.

To make a cord

Ch7, joining to form a circle with a ss. Ch2 and work 1 dc into each ch. Do not join with a ss but continue working around with 1 dc into each previous dc until desired length is reached. Finish off. You can trim the cord with rosettes and spirals.

Rosettes

A small rosette is the ideal dainty trim for the ends of ribbons or for crocheted chain ties on baby garments.

To make a rosette

Ch16.
1st row. Into 4th ch from hook work 4dc, * 5dc into next ch, rep from * to end. Finish off.
You will see the rosette forms a small curl or rose shape. The ends can be secured by a few small stitches sewn through the center. The longer the chain, and the thicker the yarn and hook which you use, the larger the rosette will be.

▼ *Tiny rosettes can be made in a few minutes and used in many ways*

Buttons

Small buttons like the ones shown are not just decorative—they're practical too! They often make a smart alternative to ordinary buttons on knitted or crocheted garments.

To make a button

Ch4, joining to form a circle with a ss.

1st round. Ch 1, work 7sc into circle. Do not join with a slip stitch. Continue in sc working * 2sc into next sc, 1 sc into each of next 2sc, rep from * 8 times. Work 1 sc into each of next 12sc. Dec by working as follows: * insert hook into next sc, yoh, draw through loop (2 loops on hook), insert hook into next sc, yoh, draw through loop (3 loops on hook), yoh, draw through all loops on hook, 1 sc into next sc, rep from * 5 times until opening is almost closed, stuffing with cotton batting as you work. Finish off and close any opening which is left.

You can vary the size of the button by increasing more or less stitches at the beginning. The number of stitches you work before decreasing will alter its depth.

▼ *Begin the button with a flat circle*   ▼ *Continue working over the filling*

Make key identification easier with crochet spirals in different shades

Spirals

You can use spirals to trim a key ring, or as a zipper tab on a sweater or a purse. Why not make a larger cluster to brighten up the ends of a scarf or cap? Or, if you're in a festive mood, work them in thicker metallic yarn and add them to a velvet ribbon—they would make a charming finishing touch to many a hair style. Make a tiny group in the finest yarn for unusual earrings.

To make a spiral

Ch20.

1st row. Work 2dc into 4th ch, * 3dc in next ch, rep * to end of ch. Cut yarn and finish off the spiral.

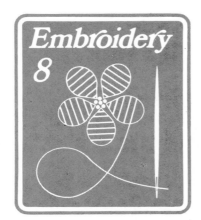

Cherry Ripe

You can add a new dimension and variety of texture to your embroidery by heightening the smooth flat surface of satin stitch with an underlayer of padding. Practice the stitch with the traditional cherry motifs in this chapter and brighten your home or wardrobe with your work. Or why not try creating your own designs with padded straight lines interspersed with whipped and laced backstitches.

Padded Stitches

Padded straight lines

To pad straight lines and stems, first cover the line of the design with small running stitches. Then cover these with a loose thread and stitch it to the fabric with small, close satin stitches. If you are working on even-weave linen, you can use the threads of the fabric as a guide for the spacing of the stitches: They should not be too crowded, nor too far apart.

Simple padding

First outline the shape with small running stitches, fill in the outline with more running stitches (chain stitch or outline stitch are also suitable for padding) and then cover with satin stitch.

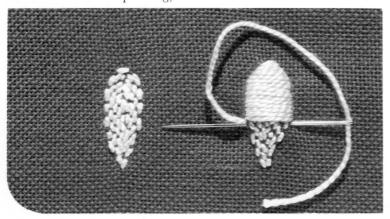

Double padding

More pronounced relief is given by padding twice. First fill in the shape with running stitches, cover with satin stitch in one direction and then work over the same area again at right angles to the first layer of satin stitch.

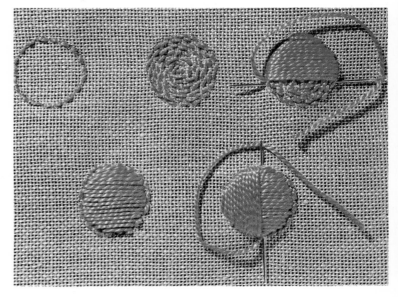

Cherry mat

You can make a colorful set of table mats and napkins, and a tablecloth with bunches of shiny ripe cherries scattered all over it, or you could embroider one beautiful bunch on a small piece of silk and mount it in an antique or old silver frame.

The cherries are worked in padded satin stitch and edged with outline stitch, the leaves in long and short stitch with veins of outline stitch. The edge of the mat is finished in buttonhole stitch, full instructions for which are given in Embroidery chapter 10, page 190.

If you would like to follow the color scheme shown here, use 6-strand embroidery floss in two shades of green, red and a touch of rust. You will find it easier to work on a firm, closely woven embroidery linen.

▼ *Actual size pattern for small cherry motif*

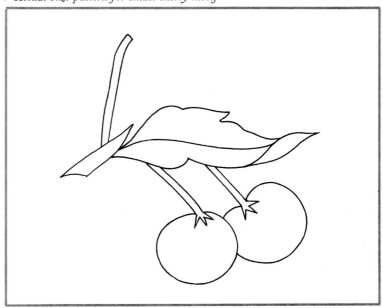

▲ *Actual size pattern for large bunch of cherries*

▼ *Table mat and napkins show a traditional use of padded satin stitch*

Collectors Piece

The Fire of London

This machine-embroidered picture by Joan Gilbert, 'Musicians Escaping from the Great Fire of London,' is based on a 17th-century engraving of the Great Fire by Visscher.

Joan Gilbert, who has held exhibitions of her embroidery, translated the engraving into appliquéd fabric, worked over richly with cotton yarn and occasional gold and silver threads. It took her about a month to work, using an automatic electric sewing machine.

In 1666, as the picture shows, there was an apple orchard at Whitefriars, surrounded by the pleasant buildings of the Carmelite monastery which were still standing.

A fine water gate with steps led down to the broad highway of the Thames. Flames and smoke fill the background and give urgency to the hurrying figures. The musicians are carrying their lutes, harps and mandolins to safety. There is also a red hurdy-gurdy, a lyre and a baryton (pronounced bar-ee-to(ng), a member of the viol family) in the rescue operation.

In the boat, a little figure in pink is gripping two big cheeses under his arms. (Cheeses could be almost as valuable as instruments— Pepys buried two cheeses in the cool river bank to avoid damage by fire.)

One fellow is carrying a bag of fine linen, and a pompous person bears away his casket full of jewels.

The lights of Hampstead can be seen through the flames.

In a sky obscured by smoke, the large gold braid stars stand still above the hullabaloo.

Instruments like those carried by the musicians can still be seen in special collections in some museums. Made of highly polished, often rare, woods, they are inlaid with bone, ivory, silver and gold.

Two details of the Fire of London picture showing some of the stitches and materials used

150

Plotting a Sunflower

Plotting the design of a rug from a chart onto the canvas requires great care. For complicated designs, such as Oriental patterns, it is easiest to buy a canvas already stenciled with the pattern. If you plot your own pattern, remember that it will show the color of the stitches in the holes, whereas the actual stitches are worked on the lines of the canvas.

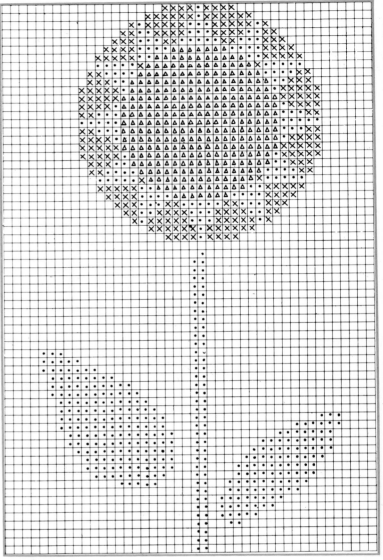

Use back of rug (left) as color key to chart—note that back of rug is in reverse position to chart. (Above) Each square represents one knot.

How to work from a chart

If you are using a chart, the process is easier if you first mark the design onto the canvas with a waterproof felt pen. Draw a vertical line down the center of the canvas from which to work the pattern. To mark the base of the stalk, count up 6 rows from the bottom of the canvas (after folding over a hem of 1½in), and mark the 2 middle holes, that is, the ones immediately on either side of the center line. Then, following the chart, count up the holes and mark the design on the canvas. It will simplify later work if the color changes on the chart are marked with a corresponding color felt pen on the canvas.

Once you have grasped the basic idea of the pattern, you can alter it to fit your own canvas. One flower, two leaves and a stalk take 1,018 holes, and 4 units of yarn. Work out the total number of holes in the canvas (width holes multiplied by length holes) and subtract from it the number of holes for each flower or flowers. The resulting background number, divided by 320, will give you the number of wool units you need in the background color. The main thing is to subtract from the total number of holes however many flowers you decide to work onto your canvas.

The sunflower rug

Working on quantities shown in Hooked Rugs chapter 1, page 132, you will need:

- ☐ Canvas 24in wide, 27in long (24in is a standard width with selvages—if you cannot find 24in-wide canvas, use a piece 27in by 27in. 27in long allows 1½in at each end to turn over).
- ☐ Yarn total 6,400 holes (80 x 80)
  red—1 unit (231 holes)
  yellow—1 unit (294 holes)
  green—2 units (493 holes)
  cream—17 units (5,382 holes)
  i.e., each flower with its leaves and stalk
  needs 4 units of wool to cover 1,018 holes
- ☐ One latchet hook
- ☐ Extra cream rug wool in a skein, not cut, for binding the edges of the finished rug (see Hooked Rugs chapter 3)
- ☐ Rug needle

▼ *A finished rug hung on the wall used as a low 'picture' beside a sofa*   ▲ *Ideas for rugs using general sunflower motifs*

Square knots are easy to make

Macramé 2

The square knot, or double knot, is another of the basic movements of macramé. It is very simple, and once you have learned how to do it, you can build up intricate braids and fabrics.

How to make a belt

This belt is made up of square knots, horizontal double half hitches and diagonal double half hitches. Set 14 double knotting threads onto the shank of a buckle. Work a row of horizontal double half hitches. * Using square knots work 7 braids, followed by 2 rows of horizontal double half hitches. With the center 12 threads work diagonal double half hitches. Work braids on the remaining threads. Work 2 rows of horizontal double half hitches.* Repeat from * to * for the length required. Darn the threads into the back of the work and trim them off.

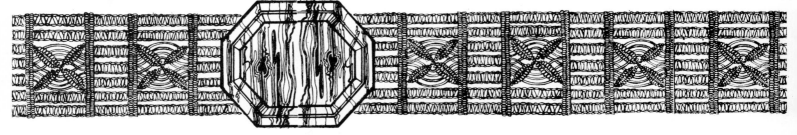

Square knots

Set on threads in multiples of four, and work a line of double half hitches. The center two threads of each group of four act as a core over which the right- and left-hand threads are knotted. Hold the two center threads taut in your left hand by winding them around the third finger.

With your right hand, form the right-hand thread into a loop with the end passing under the center core and over the left-hand thread.

Then bring the left-hand thread over the core and thread it through the loop from the front of the work.

Pull both threads up until the knot closes tightly around the center core. This completes the first part of the knot. Repeat the process in reverse order, forming the left-hand thread into a loop and passing the right-hand thread as shown in the illustrations.

This double knot forms the basis of many different braids. By alternating the arrangement of the knots by working in consecutive rows you can also build them up into durable, attractive fabric.

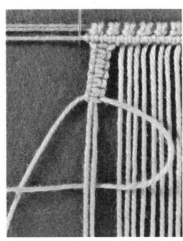

1. Loop right-hand thread under

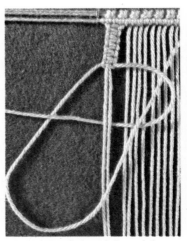

2. Left-hand thread through loop

3. Pull both threads to close knot

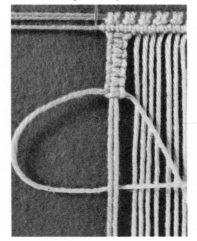

4. Make loop with left-hand thread

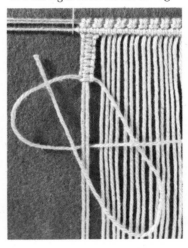

5. Pass right-hand thread through

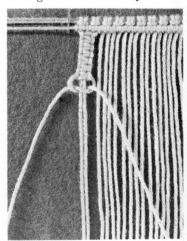

6. Tighten threads to complete knot

Alternating square knots

You can make a lovely pattern by using this method—and it's not so difficult as it may look.

Set on the threads in multiples of four, as wide or as narrow as you like, and work a row of square knots.

In the second row leave the first two threads loose and work a square knot with the next four threads, using two threads from the knot above and two from the next knot along. Keep on doing this until you reach the end of the row. You will have two threads over. Leave these loose.

Work the third row in exactly the same way as the first, the fourth the same as the second. Just keep on repeating these two rows until you have as much "fabric" as you need.

Square knot on six threads

This is a more complicated version of the square knot, but it produces a superb effect as you can see. It is worked on groups of six threads and needs a bit of concentration.

To make fabric, set on threads to the required width.

For the first group work a knot with the middle four threads in the usual way. Then, using the two outside threads, work another knot using the four middle threads as a core. Complete the process with another square knot like the first, worked with the four middle threads. (It may sound confusing when you read it for the first time, but when you actually work it, you will be able to do it with ease.) Continue for the entire row.

In the second row, leave the first three threads loose, then use the next six for the first knot, combining the last three threads of the knot above with the first three threads of the next knot above. Continue to the end of the row, leaving the last three threads loose. The third row is the same as the first, so all you do is alternate the first two rows until the fabric reaches the length you need.

Carry on with a tote bag

Coarse string would be ideal to use for this easy bag, but make sure it's a smooth twisted string, or it could be rough on your hands. Once you have worked it in string (remember this also has the advantage that it just grows and grows—visibly) you could use the idea scaled down to make a small evening bag in a finer thread with bangle bracelets for handles.

Buy two handles (wooden or plastic rings or bangles). Set threads onto each. Work following the instructions for alternating square knots or square knots on six threads or, if you like, the diagonal half hitch pattern covered in Macramé chapter 1, page 134.

After a few inches, join the two sections at the sides, and continue the work as a sort of circular tube, until the bag reaches the length you want. To finish off, knot the threads together on the inside of the bag, and trim ends.

▲ *Braid with alternating square knots* ▼ *and square knots in sets of 6 threads*

Stitch detail of tote bag, shown right, worked in square knots

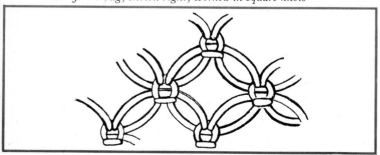

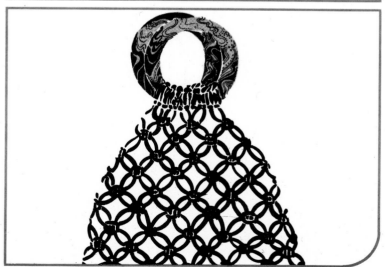

155

Fine finishes

So far in Creative Hands only one method has been given for finishing the waist seam of a skirt, but there are many other ways of doing this. Each method is designed to do a specific job, so that once you know how to use the various finishes, you will be able to adapt them to your personal needs. Some fabrics dictate the way in which they must be finished, but the waistbands described here can be used successfully on all the fabrics suggested for skirts in Dressmaking chapter 4, page 76, and are the most commonly used.

The waistband with enclosed stiffening

First, make a paper pattern for the waistband.

To work out how long to cut the waistband, measure your waist and add 2in for wrap.

The stiffening, which can be either belting or grosgrain ribbon, should be 1in wide, and the waistband must be twice as wide as the stiffening, plus $\frac{1}{4}$in. The $\frac{1}{4}$in is taken up when the waistband is turned over the top of the stiffening.

So, for a size 26in waist, the pattern will be 28in by $2\frac{1}{4}$in.

Don't add ease to the waistband unless you like it loose.

Lay the pattern on single fabric. If you use a strip of fabric from the side of the skirt layout, check the grain lines. In many fabrics the fact that the grain on the waistband runs in a different direction from the skirt does not matter, but if the fabric you are using has a marked grain, it is a point to watch.

Pin the pattern onto the fabric and mark around it with long, flat basting stitches.

Add $\frac{3}{4}$in seam allowance all around and cut out.

How to mark out the fabric waistband

WRAP	BACK	FRONT

Basting and stitching

The wrap of a waistband always goes on the back of the skirt and tucks under the front fastening, to line up with the side seam. With the right side of the fabric facing you, mark off 2in from the left seamline and then mark the center between this point and the right seamline. With right sides facing, raw edges even, place the waistband to the skirt and pin, letting the wrap extend over the opening. Baste and sew in place.

Cut the belting or other stiffening exactly to the length of the waistband pattern, that is, with wrap but without seam allowance. Again, mark off 2in from the left and find the center of the rest. Pin and baste the belting over the seam allowance of waistband and skirt with the bottom edge of the stiffening just meeting stitching line. Stitch in position along edge of stiffening.

Fold seam allowance over the stiffening at each end, making the front edge even with the zipper opening, and baste. Fold waistband over the stiffening and turn under the seam allowance along the lower edge on the inside of the skirt. Pin and baste to skirt along the stitching line. Hand sew into position with firm stitches and slip stitch turned-in ends to close. Remove basting.

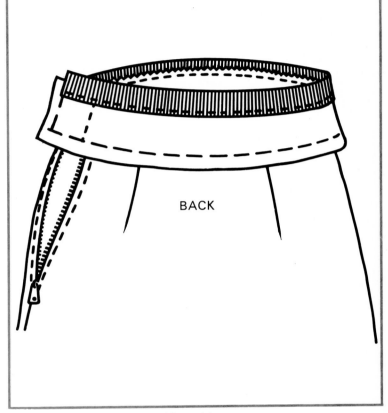

The belting or stiffening stitched in position

Attaching hooks and eyes

The hook and eye fastening for this type of waistband is slightly different from the one used for the flared skirt.

Using two hooks and one eye, first sew one of the hooks to the front edge of the waistband, about $\frac{1}{4}$in from the end, and make a bar by hand on the back of the waistband, even with the zipper opening, as shown on the opposite page.

When the zipper is closed, with the wrap tucked underneath, the waistband will fasten in line with the side seam.

How to make a bar

The bar sewn by hand goes across the center of the back of the waistband, in line with the hook, and is sewn from the top toward the bottom.

Thread a needle with strong machine twist to match the skirt, pull it double and make a knot at the end. Insert the needle from the back and return it into the fabric about $\frac{1}{2}$in farther down, placing the tip of your thumb nail under the thread as you pull it through to prevent it from becoming too tight. This tack makes the foundation of the bar.

Now return the needle to the top of the tack and repeat the stitch four times, being careful not to pull the thread tight at the back. Then, before you make the buttonhole stitch, work over the back threads and whip them firmly down to the fabric to prevent the bar from stretching.

Buttonhole stitch over the tacks, as shown in the photograph, keeping the tip of your thumb-nail under the threads to avoid

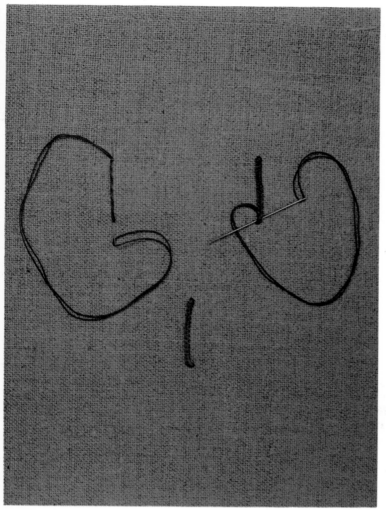

Making the bar

catching the fabric in the stitches. Make the stitches as close together as possible without overlapping them, and fasten them off at the back when you have completed the bar. If the knot at the back of your work is unsightly, cut it off now.

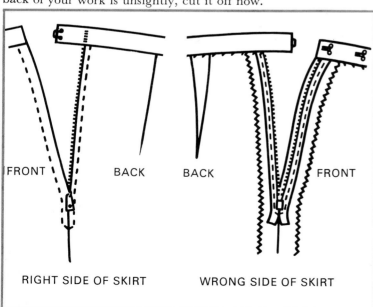

FRONT   BACK   BACK   FRONT

RIGHT SIDE OF SKIRT   WRONG SIDE OF SKIRT

The finished waistband with correct setting for the hooks, eyes, and bar

Finishing the fastening

Sew the eye to the edge of the wrap, on top of the waistband and not underneath it, leaving the eye extending as shown.

To find the correct position for the second hook, close the zipper and the hook and bar, and place the second hook on the inside of the front waistband $\frac{1}{8}$in farther in from the eye.

When you sew the hooks, eye and bar into position, make sure that the stitch catches through to the stiffening for extra hold, but do not stitch through to the outside. It is important not to place the second hook 2in from the front edge of the waistband (the length of the wrap) because, depending on the thickness of the fabric, this measurement sometimes alters slightly and the fastening might stretch. The strain would then break the hand-made bar, which only holds the top of the waistband down.

Hangers for this waistband can be either one of the types described in Dressmaking chapter 7, page 136.

The soft waistband

So far the two most popular methods of making a stiff waistband have been covered, but you may prefer one without stiffening which is soft and less constricting.

This type of waistband should not be deeper than 1in, because it would turn over at the top. And, for extra support, the waist seam allowance on the skirt must be the same as the width of the waistband, or else it will wrinkle. It will also wrinkle if it is too tight, so the soft waistband must fit around you less snugly than the stiff waistband.

Using the previously prepared pattern, add 1in ease and work exactly as before, leaving out the stiffening.

The hidden waistband

The waistbands made so far are visible and are fixed to the top of the skirt. This type of waistband is hidden, and the best materials to use are either belting or stiff grosgrain ribbon.

Since this waistband is not supported by fabric, it is advisable to use a wider belting than you have used for the others. The best width to work on is $1\frac{1}{2}$in.

This type of waistband must be curved and fit to the body.

To obtain the curve

Don't pleat the belting, since this only results in an unsightly kink in the waist seam, but use the following method:

Cut the belting to the length you require for your waist measurement plus 5in. Lay it flat on an ironing board and press over the belting with a hot iron and damp cloth. Before the steam

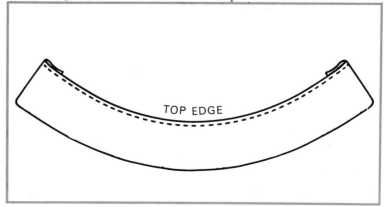

TOP EDGE

The belting, correctly curved, and ready to use

has dried remove the cloth and gently pull the lower edge of the belting into a curve. Dry off the dampness on the belting with a hot iron, fixing the shape and pressing in the fullness around the top edge. To prevent this edge from stretching when you attach it to the skirt, run a stay stitch through it on the sewing machine, feeding it into the machine from the front and letting it run out behind the needle, without pulling it.

Now measure the inner curve to the length that you need for your waist size. Add 1in at each end, and cut off the rest. Turn under each end ½in, then fit the band to your waist. It should lie around your body closely but not tightly.

Basting and stitching to the skirt

Take out the marking for the original seam allowance of ¾in on the skirt waist seam, and mark a new line ⅜in from the top edge. This is necessary because, as you turn the waistband under, it will take up some of the length. This would make your fitting incorrect. Following the sketch, lay the short, inner curve of the belting to the inside of the new waist seam line and stitch into position close to the edge of the belting.

Cut a length of straight seam binding in a matching color, ½in shorter than the top edge of the belting, and lay it over the raw

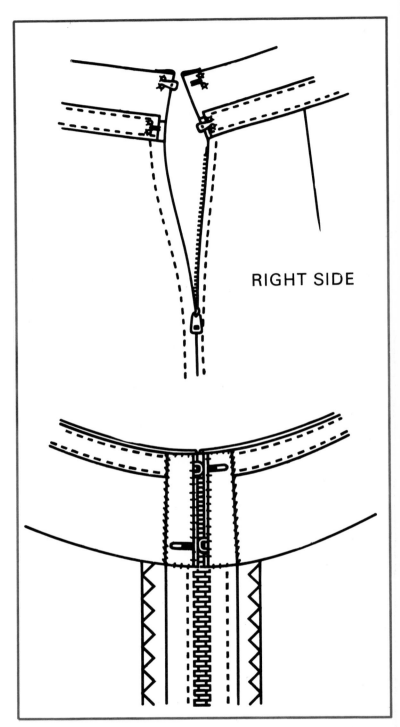

RIGHT SIDE

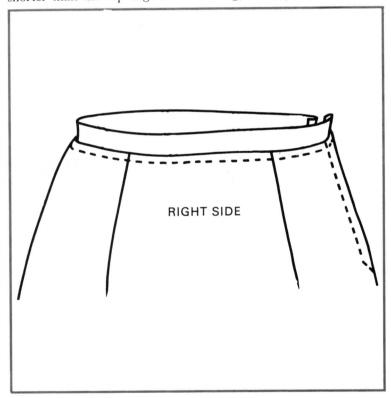

RIGHT SIDE

The curved belting stitched to the inside of the waist seam

waist edge on the right side of the skirt and the belting, leaving ¼in at each end uncovered.

The lower edge of the seam binding must cover the row of stitches. Baste and stitch into position along both edges of the seam binding.

Hooks and eyes

To fasten this waistband, use hooks and eyes on the edges of the waistband opening and place a hook to an eye and an eye to a hook. Since the waistband must not fit tightly into the waist, this method will insure that they cannot come undone. They must be sewn to what is now the outside of the waistband, which is later tucked in, otherwise the top hook could not be done up when the skirt is finished.

Above: the hook and eye setting for the hidden waistband with seam binding covering the raw edges
Below: hidden waistband fastening with finished edges, seen from inside

Now turn the belting and seam binding to the inside of the skirt and baste along the upper edge. To finish off the edges, cut two strips of seam binding 2½in long. Turn under ½in at each end and sew them over the edges of the waistband, covering the raw edges at the top, and passing them under the hook-bars as shown in the diagram. Slip stitch in place all around. If the skirt fabric is heavy, you may find it an advantage to machine stitch along the folded edge at the top of the skirt, to prevent the waistband from working up over the top. On normal skirt-weight fabric, though, it should be enough to attach the bottom edge of the belting in a few places, such as the seams and darts, with a light holding stitch.

Hangers

If you want to make skirt hangers for this waistband, use the flat type as described in Dressmaking chapter 7, page 136. Ideally this waist finish should hang on a spring-loaded skirt hanger, however, otherwise the skirt may pull out of shape.

Zipper in a straight seam

Although the overlap type of zipper opening (the one used on the simple flared skirt) is the most commonly used in side seams on skirts, you may wish to put a zipper into the center back or center front seam of a skirt. In this case, the zipper will have to be stitched in so that the stitching lines are equal on both sides.

Prepare the opening by basting the seams together and pressing them carefully, as for the side seams.

Remove the basting. Open the zipper to the bottom, and lay it in the skirt opening so that the seam edges just cover the zipper teeth on both sides. Baste the zipper into position.

To make sure that the seams lie perfectly flat and don't push each other up, close the zipper before you machine stitch it in.

If the seams do push up, take the seam edges back a fraction until they lie flat, still keeping the zipper completely hidden. Start stitching about $\frac{3}{8}$in from the seam edge on one side and stitch down until you are even with the zipper end. To make the miter at the end, turn the work and stitch toward the seam. Pivot the work on the needle and return on the other side in the same way.

This method of inserting a zipper is most successful when it's used on a straight seam. But for a curved seam, the overlap on one side is safer, since the equal distance of the stitching line on both sides —down into and then up into the grain, over the rigid tape of the zipper—would tend to drag the seam and make it twist.

Since skirt zippers are always of the heavier variety, it is not advisable to insert them by hand, except in very fine fabrics where you would use a dress-weight zipper. This is covered in a later chapter.

A word about the invisible zipper

To insert this type, you must have the right zipper foot for your sewing machine to enable you to put in the zipper properly. Carefully follow instructions to get the correct finish. Without the correct foot the result will not be satisfactory.

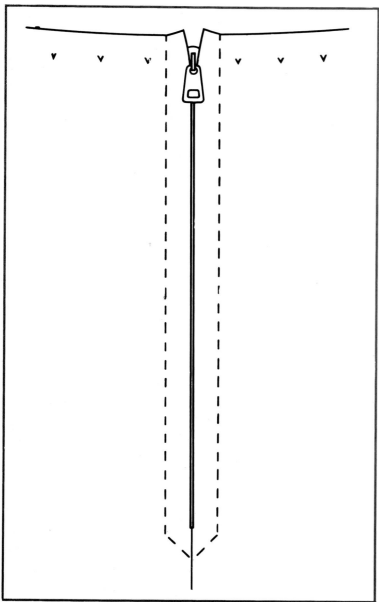

Zipper stitched in a straight seam

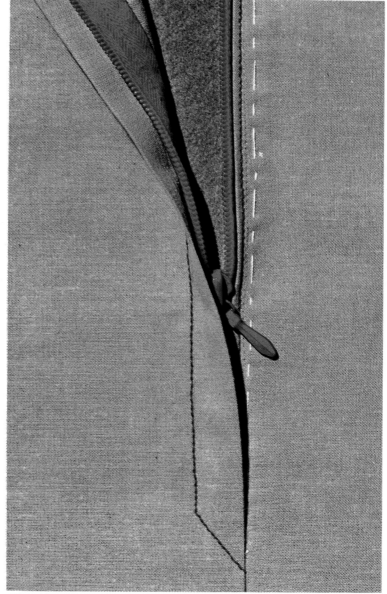

Zipper in a curved seam

Fashion Flair

Casual belts

Know how to give a ready-made belt a custom-made look? Just add decorations and designs of your own, as these sketches show. The results may look expensive, but the cost of materials is very little. Unusual buttons, exotic braids, colorful beads, sequins and even drapery tassels can all transform an ordinary belt into an eye-catching creation. You will soon find inspiration from those 'odds and ends' you have been saving! Remnants of leather or felt, or pieces of crochet work can be cut into clever shapes as appliqués or tacked together for a patchwork effect. Larger pieces of material can be made into loop-through pockets. Look through fashion magazines for ideas—then launch out with your own variations.

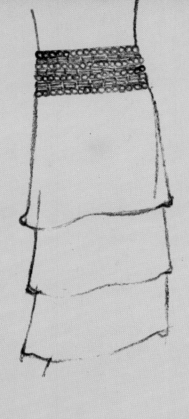

Beads saved from an old bead curtain can be used to make a bold evening belt

Slotted ribbons, sequins and beads can be added to a simple fabric belt to give an expensive look

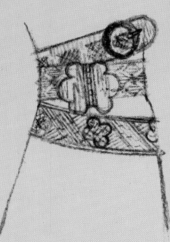

Simple leather belts can have stuck and stitched pieces of leather and felt added to give them a touch of originality

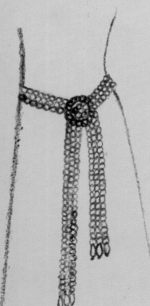

Beads strung together to form long strips make an attractive belt when slotted through a jewelled buckle

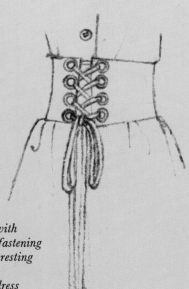

A wide belt with eyelet slotted fastening makes an interesting finish for a simple shirt dress

Crochet can be used on a belt by applying motifs to a fabric belt or by crocheting a belt strip and even adding a pocket

Cross-stitch diamonds

You will enjoy stitching this piece of needlepoint—it is gay, colorful and worked completely in simple cross-stitch. Use it to make any of the things already mentioned in the needlepoint chapters, or how about making a door stop? Just work a piece large enough to cover the top and sides of an ordinary brick and use felt for the ends and the base.

You can work this design in tapestry, crewel or knitting yarns, but if you would like to copy the color scheme in the illustration, use tapestry yarn in rose, pink, bright blue and light yellow. For this yarn you will need a tapestry needle size No.19.

The picture shows the design very much enlarged but the actual size of the section illus-trated will measure about 4 inches square when worked on double-thread canvas with 10 double threads to the inch. Worked on single-weave canvas with 18 threads to 1 inch, the section will cover an area of about $4\frac{1}{2}$ inches square. Work cross-stitch over 2 double threads each way on double-thread canvas and over 4 threads each way on single-thread canvas.

Double increasing & decreasing

Double increasing in knitting is where two stitches are made as a pair, usually at either side of a central point. Double decreasing is where two stitches are taken out of the work. While both double increasing and decreasing may be used just for shaping, they may also have very stunning decorative uses. They are essential, for example, if you want to make a lacy pattern or create the zigzag designs and stripes which produce the chevron effect illustrated below.

Double increasing

Purled double increase

This method uses a central stitch and is worked on stockinette stitch. Knit up to one stitch before the center stitch. Knit into that

Striped chevron pattern using double increases and decreases

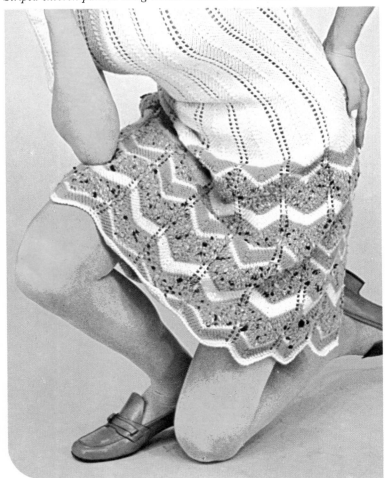

stitch, but before slipping it off the needle purl into the yarn in the row immediately below from the back of the work. Slip the original stitches off the left-hand·needle. Knit the center stitch. Knit the next stitch, but again purl into the back of the stitch below before slipping the stitch off the needle. Purl all the stitches on the next row.

Twisted double increase

Again a central stitch is used and the increased stitches are on either side of it.

Work to one stitch before the center stitch. Knit into the front and then into the back of this stitch. Knit the center stitch. Knit into the front and then the back of the next stitch. Purl all stitches on the next row.

Crossed double increase

With this method, both stitches to be increased are worked into the center stitch.

Knit to the center stitch. Knit into the row below the center stitch, knit the center stitch and knit again into the row below the center stitch. Purl all the stitches on the next row.

Double decreasing

The simple double decrease

Probably the most commonly used pair of double decreases are those made by working three stitches together.

Knitting three stitches together (K3tog) gives you a right-slanting decrease.

Knitting three stitches together through the back of the loops (K3tog tbl) gives you a left-slanting decrease.

A neater form of this left-slanting decrease is to slip the first stitch and then the second stitch from left- to right-hand needle. Knit the next stitch. With the left-hand needle point, lift both slipped stitches over the knitted stitch.

The slipped decrease

This decrease is worked over three stitches. Slip the first stitch onto the right-hand needle. Knit the next two stitches together and, with the left-hand needle, lift the slipped stitch over the stitch made by knitting two together. This slants to the left.

The right-slanting version of this decrease is used much less frequently and directions for working it are usually given in full when it does occur.

Slip the first stitch onto the right-hand needle. Knit the next stitch and, with left-hand needle point, lift the slipped stitch over the knitted stitch and off the needle. Put the knitted stitch back onto the left-hand needle and lift the next stitch over it with the right-hand needle point. Return the knitted stitch to the right-hand needle.

A double decrease worked on the purl side of the work

This decrease is worked on the purl, or wrong side, of stockinette stitch and slants to the left on the knit side of the work. Purl two together (P2tog) and return to the left-hand needle. With the right-hand needle point, lift the second stitch on the left-hand needle over the first and then return the first stitch to the right-hand needle.

The reverse of this (slanting to the right on the knit side of the work) is worked by slipping one stitch onto the right-hand needle. Knit the next stitch, then twist the following one by reversing it on the needle, leaving it on the left-hand needle. Return the knitted stitch to the left-hand needle with the right-hand needle point and lift the twisted stitch over it. Return the knitted stitch to the right-hand needle.

Purled double increase

Twisted double increase

Crossed double increase

Simple double decrease: ▲ *K3tog* ▼ *K3tog tbl*

Slipped decrease: ▲ *slip stitch over K2tog* ▼ *lift second slip stitch over*

The ribbed turtleneck pullover

Even for the relative beginner, this classic ribbed turtleneck knits up easily and, of course, would make an ideal gift for either a boy or a girl. Work it in the traditional camel or white, as illustrated, or choose any other color to suit your taste. If you've forgotten some of the abbreviations used here, look back to Knitting Know-how chapter 1, page 7.

Sizes

Directions are for 32in bust or chest.
Length down center back, 23½ [23¾:24:24¼]in.
Sleeve seam 17½in.
The figures in brackets [] refer to the 34, 36 and 38in sizes respectively.

Gauge
for this design
6sts and 8 rows to 1in on No.5 needles.

Materials
Sports yarn
10 [12:12:14] ounces
One pair No. 3 needles
or Canadian No. 10
One pair No. 5 needles
or Canadian No. 8
2 stitch holders

Abbreviations
Look back to Knitting Know-How chapter 1, page 7. to refresh your memory.

Note
For a truly professional finished look, use the invisible binding off method for completing the collar. Directions for this are given in Knitting Know-how chapter 6.

164

Back

Using No.3 needles cast on 96 [102:108:114] sts.
1st row K2, P4 [P1:P4:K3, P4], * K4, P4, rep from * to last 2 [5:0:3] sts, K2 [K4, P1: 0:K3].
2nd row P2, K4 [K1:K4: P3, K4], * P4, K4, rep from * to last 2 [5:0:3] sts, P2 [P4, K1:0:P3].
These 2 rows form the rib and are rep throughout back.
Work 22 rows more.
Change to No.5 needles and continue in rib.
Work until 98 rows from beg, or desired length to armholes.

Shape armholes
Bind off 1[2:3:4] sts at beg of next 2 rows.
Dec one st at each end of next and every other row until 82 [82:86:86] sts rem.
Work 41 [39:41:39] rows without shaping.

Shape shoulders
1st row K2, sl1, K1, psso, rib to last 4sts, K2 tog, K2.
2nd row P2, P2 tog, rib to last 4sts, P2 tog tbl, P2.
Rep last 2 rows 8 [8:9:9] times, then first row once.
Leave rem 46sts on holder.

Front

Using No.3 needles cast on 110 [116:122:128] sts.
1st row K1 [K4:P3, K4: K2], * P4, K4, rep from * to last 5 [0:3:6:] sts, P4, K1 [0:P3:P4, K2].
2nd row P1 [P4:K3, P4: P2], *K4, P4, rep from * to last 5 [0:3:6] sts, K4, P1 [0:K3: K4, P2].

Work 22 rows more in rib.
Change to No.5 needles and continue in rib.
Work until 98 rows from beg, or until same desired length as back.

Shape armholes
Bind off 4 [5:6:7] sts at beg of next 2 rows.
Dec one st at each end of next 6 [8:8:10] rows.
Work 44 [44:46:46] rows without shaping.

Shape shoulders
Bind off 19 [19:21:21] sts at beg of next 2 rows.
Leave rem sts on holder for neck.

Sleeves

Using No.3 needles cast on 54 [56:58:60] sts.
1st row P1 [2:3:4], K4, *P4, K4, rep from * to last 1 [2:3:4] sts, P1 [2:3:4].
2nd row K1 [2:3:4], P4, *K4, P4, rep from * to last 1 [2:3:4] sts, K1 [2:3:4].
Continue in rib for 22 rows more.
Change to No.5 needles and continue in rib, working extra sts into rib pattern as they are added. Work 2 rows.
Inc 1 st at each end of next and every 8th row until there are 80 [84:88:92] sts.
Work until sleeve measures 17½in or desired length, ending with a WS row.

Shape cap
1st row K2, sl1, K1, psso, rib to last 4sts, K2 tog, K2.
2nd row P2, P2 tog, rib to last 4sts, P2 tog tbl, P2.
Rep last 2 rows twice.
7th row as 1st.
8th row P3, rib to last 3sts, P3.
Rep 7th and 8th rows until 32 sts rem.
Repeat 1st and 2nd rows 3 times.
Bind off.

Collar

Sew left shoulder seam.
Using No.5 needles rib across sts from back and front holders (96 sts). Work 43 rows in rib. Bind off.

Finishing

Sew collar and right shoulder seam.
Sew side and sleeve seams.
Set in sleeves.
Press lightly using a damp cloth with a cool iron.

These pullovers have been specially designed to look good on a boy or a girl, since the elasticity of the rib allows for contours! The continental shaping which has been used is of particular interest and is actually simpler to do, with better results, than the standard American type of shaping. It gives a close-fitting look, letting the clear lines of the rib reach over the shoulder from the front to the sloping back seam. The shoulder seam itself is set behind the shoulder.

Sweaters for boys or girls ►
▼ Stitch detail of rib

Crochet Know-how 9

Distinctively Different

In this age of standardized clothes and mass production, it is easy enough to find your best friend wearing the same dress as your own. Accessories are the best way to add individual touches of character, but any which are the least out of the ordinary can be really costly—so why not try to make them yourself? Ties, belts, watchbands or hatbands all lend a finishing touch and can give your outfits a more personalized look. Give your imagination free rein and once you start toning, matching or mixing yarn textures as well as colors, you will find the possibilities are endless. Try using a thick wool yarn to make a chunky hatband or work a fine watchband or belt in glittering metallic yarn for evening wear. Cashmere gives an elegant touch to a tie, and a matching tie and hatband set could be particularly lovely in angora. By the way, with the appropriate color and yarn choice, all these ideas make acceptable presents for men too.

The instructions for making the accessories illustrated (plus a belt) are set out here. They have been specially designed for speedy and easy working, but simply by altering the length and width you can tailor the instructions to suit your own needs.

For each design you will need:
- ☐ 1 ball in each of 3 colors of Coats & Clark's O.N.T. Speed Cro-Sheen
- ☐ 1 No.0 steel crochet hook
- ☐ 1 buckle for belt
- ☐ 1 small buckle for watchband

Watchband

With main color, ch3. Turn.
1st row. 1 sc into 2nd ch, 1 sc into next ch. Turn.
2nd row. Ch 1, 1 sc into next sc, 1 sc into turning ch. Turn. Rep 2nd row until work is 9in long. Cut yarn and finish off. Beg working around sides and ends of band.
1st round. With 1st contrast join to right-hand corner of end with ss, ch2, 1 sc into same space, ch1 (1 sc, ch1) twice into next st. Work along side to other corner as follows: *skip 1 sp, 1 sc into next sp, ch 1, rep from * to corner. (1 sc, ch 1) twice into next 2 sp. Work along second side as given for first side, joining to first ch with a ss. Cut yarn and finish off.
2nd round. With 2nd contrast join to center of corner sts with ss. Work as given for first round, keeping extra corner sts in center of round ends.
3rd round. As 2nd. Cut yarn and finish off. Sew buckle to one end.

166

Hatband

Work as for watchband, repeating 2nd row until work is 24in long. Work 1st and 2nd rounds. Then work one more round of 1st contrast and two of main color.

Tie

With main color work center band as for watchband until your work is 46in long. Continue as follows.
1st round. With 1st contrast as for watchband.
2nd round. With 2nd contrast join with ss 16in from one end. Work around end to 16in along other side in same way as for 1st round. Cut yarn and finish last st as a ss. Finish off.

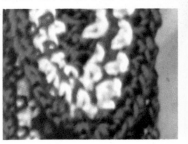

▲ *Close-up showing the rounded end of the tie*

With 2nd contrast join in the same way 11in from other end and work around end to 11in along other side. Finish off.
3rd round. With 1st contrast work as for 2nd round, beg 11in from one end and 9½in from other end.
4th and 5th rounds. With main color work as given for 1st round of watchband. Finish off ends.

Belt

With main color work as for watchband. Continue until 6in longer than desired waist measurement.
1st round. As for watchband.
2nd round. As 1st round with 2nd contrast.
3rd round. As 1st round with 1st contrast.
4th and 5th rounds. As 1st round with main color. Finish off ends. Sew buckle to one end.

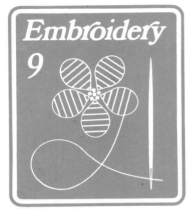

Embroidery in chains

Chain stitch gives an even, regular line, perfect for outlines and for flowing twists and turns. When worked in close rows, it also makes a good filling stitch.

Chain stitch

Work from the top down, making a chain of loops on the right side of the material and a line of backstitches at the back. Bring the needle through on the line of the design and hold the thread down with the left thumb. Insert the needle again at the point where it first emerged and bring the needle out a bit farther along the line.

Pull the needle through, keeping the thread under the point so that the next stitch holds it down in a loop. Continue working in the same way for the length of chain required.

Backstitched chain

Backstitched chain is a very simple variation, worked with a row of backstitches over each of the chain stitches.

Zigzag chain stitch

Work this in the same way as simple chain stitch, but work each stitch at an angle to the one before it to form a

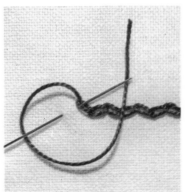

zigzag. Pierce the end of each loop before you take the needle through the fabric so that the loops stay in place.

Russian chain stitch

Make a chain stitch. Then, instead of continuing in a straight line, make the next stitch at an angle pointing to the left, then another to the right, catching each down with a tiny stitch. Bring the needle out again farther along the line

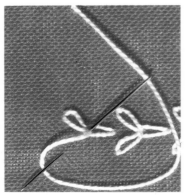

and repeat to make a line of stitches. This stitch can also be worked in groups as a filling stitch, or lined up in horizontal rows.

Whipped chain stitch

Chain stitch can be whipped to give it greater effect. Work either a single line, or two or three lines together, and whip with a contrasting thread for a braided effect.

Cable chain stitch

Start with a simple chain stitch. Then, holding the thread down with your left thumb, pass the needle under the thread and twist the needle into a vertical position so that the point comes over the thread. Insert the needle into the fabric so that the working thread is twisted around it, and make another chain stitch.

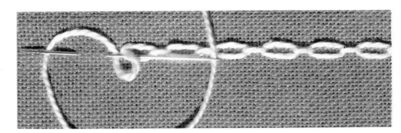

Detached chain stitch

Make a chain stitch, then make a tiny stitch to hold the loop down. Leave a space and bring the needle out again to begin to make the next stitch.

Daisy chain stitch (or lazy-daisy stitch)

This is worked in the same way as for detached chain stitch, but the detached chain is placed to form a flower shape.

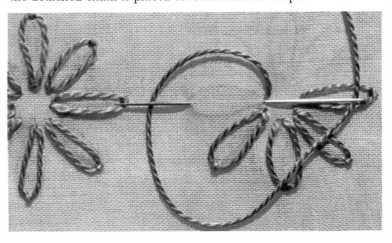

Heavy chain stitch

First make a small running stitch at A, then bring the needle out just below it at B. Thread the needle back under the running stitch and insert it again at B. Take another small stitch below at C, then thread the needle again under

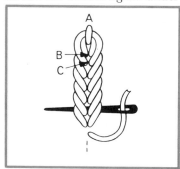

the first running stitch. Continue making the third and following stitches in the same way, always threading the needle under two stitches.

Twisted chain stitch

For this stitch variation the needle is inserted at an angle

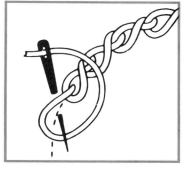

to form the twist as shown in the diagram, giving a slightly raised line.

Checkered chain stitch

Checkered chain stitch is another version. Simply thread

two yarns of different colors through the needle and use them for alternate stitches.

Platyloma calomelanas is the fourth in the Creative Hands set of eight ferns. The stitches in this chapter cover all the chain stitch variations in the complete set — the remaining four ferns are featured in Embroidery chapter 11, page 208. Fern No. 4: Platyloma calomelanas, shows zigzag chain stitch used for one of the stems.

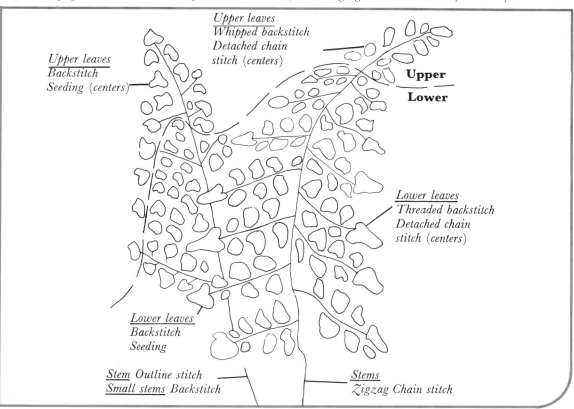

Upper leaves
Whipped backstitch
Detached chain stitch (centers)

Upper leaves
Backstitch
Seeding (centers)

Upper

Lower

Lower leaves
Threaded backstitch
Detached chain stitch (centers)

Lower leaves
Backstitch
Seeding

Stem Outline stitch
Small stems Backstitch

Stems
Zigzag Chain stitch

Collector's Piece

Elizabethan pillow cover

Today we cover up our pillows with a bedspread, but the Elizabethans, it seems, intended their pillows to show. They embroidered delicious, garden-encrusted covers, called 'pillow beres', for each pillow. The one illustrated here is part of a set in the Abingdon Collection at the Victoria and Albert Museum, London. The average size of these pillow cases was 35in by 20in. They were always made of white linen and their backs were plain and attached by open seams trimmed with herringbone stitch. Unlike cushion covers of the same period, pillow covers are nearly always without a border. Such covers ceased to be made in the 17th century as the fashion had developed for embroidered draperies.

The flowers and fruits are those found in an Elizabethan garden, usually embroidered in their natural colors—carnation, rose, pansy, pomegranate, borage, pear, honeysuckle, campion and oak. Illuminators used them to decorate their manuscripts and calendars together with birds and small animals, providing models for the embroiderers to copy.

In the cover illustrated here, silk, silver and silver gilt threads have been used, but the stitchery has been kept simpler and flatter than much of the same sort of work found on Elizabethan garments. The stitches are all a variation on chain and buttonhole.

Photograph by courtesy of
the Victoria & Albert Museum, London.

Ceylon stitch

Open Ceylon stitch

Detached buttonhole filling—
taking the needle through a
different loop from usual

Left—chain stitch
Right—chain stitch—double

Left—buttonhole stitch
Right—detached buttonhole filling

Fancy buttonhole filling, smaller
and firmer than the other and
not worked over a ladder of
threads made beforehand

Fringes and finishes

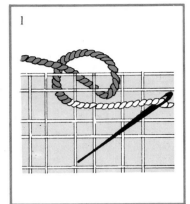

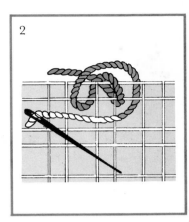

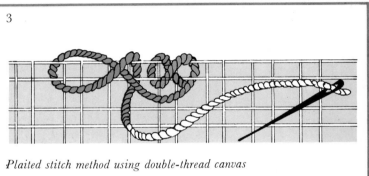

Plaited stitch method using double-thread canvas

A lot of work goes into a rug and it is meant to take a lot of wear and tear, especially at the edges. Knowing how to finish and strengthen these edges correctly will do more than anything' to preserve a rug's good looks. Otherwise, the outside tufts soon tend to lie down and the selvages quickly begin to wear away. Cut lengths of yarn are only used for the tufts of a rug—for finishing the edges you will need skeins of matching rug yarn. If a rug, or part of a rug, has already been worked, it is still possible to finish the edges at a later stage as long as one hole of rug canvas has been left free on each side for turning in the selvages. If you are just beginning to work a rug with a patterned design, play safe by working the edging stitch along one end only and up part of the sides. Make sure that the pattern will be symmetrical and quite complete before you finish the other edges. If you don't, you may have the frustrating task of picking the work apart to correct any miscalculations. Two special edging stitch methods are covered in this chapter, one worked with a needle and one with a crochet hook, as well as an attractive fringed finish—just choose the one you think is most suitable for your particular rug.

Plaited stitch method

Of the several stitches you can use to finish the edges securely, plaited stitch is usually the best one. It is simple and quick to do and, at the same time, is attractive to look at. Incidentally, it is easy to repair whenever accidents or wear and tear take their toll. Plaited stitch is just as suitable for finishing the needle-made rugs described in later chapters.

How to work plaited stitch

This stitch is worked from right to left. Work with the cut edge folded uppermost overlapping about five holes, and the selvages turned in tightly, so that you sew over only half their width.
1. Bring the needle through from the back of the canvas, leaving about three inches of yarn as a tail lying along the top edge where it can be held by your left hand. This will be covered by the stitches as you go along. Then, take the needle over the edge to the back again and bring it through one hole to the left.
2. Take the needle over the edge and back through the first hole.
3. Take the needle over the edge again and bring it from back to front through the third hole to the left. Take it over the edge for the final time and bring it through the second hole to the right. Continue, moving forward three holes and back two, remembering that the needle should always pass from the back to the front of the canvas. On reaching the left-hand corner go back two, forward two, back one, forward one, and then continue around the selvage, starting again with step 1.

The crochet edging stitch

Use a No. J (6.00 mm.) crochet hook. Fold over the cut edges of your canvas and selvages as for plaited stitch.
Work from right to left.
1. Push the crochet hook through the first hole and pull back a loop of yarn, leaving a long tail which you can darn in afterward.
2. With the loop still on the crochet hook, catch the yarn from the back over the top of the canvas and pull it through the loop.
3. Put the crochet hook through the next hole and catch the yarn from the back and pull it through the hole.
4. Then catching the yarn again from over the top, pull it through the two loops already on the hook.
5. Push the hook through the third hole and continue repeating steps 3 and 4. To join the yarn, always leave a long end from your first ball and from the new ball to darn in afterward.

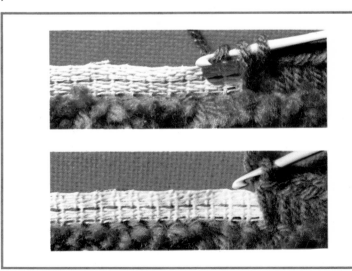

A hooked, Persian-style rug with plaited stitch edging

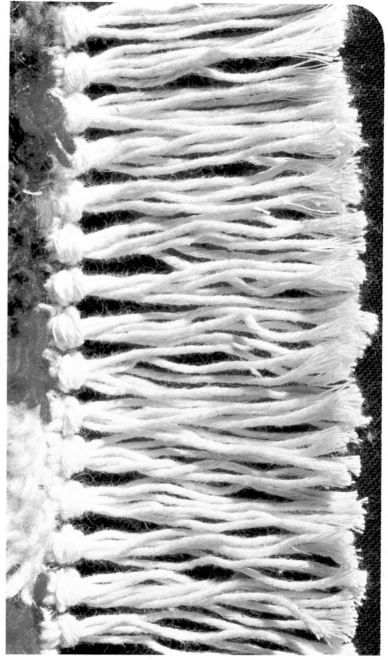

Attractive cotton fringe, using three strands of cotton for each tassel

Fringe

Fringe is always attractive and helps to add extra inches to the length of your rug. Originally this was the cut and knotted warp threads from a rug woven on a loom, but there is a quick and easy way to add a fringe to your canvas foundation and you can vary the colors as you wish. Cotton thread is sturdy and gives your rug a professional look.

How to make a fringe

It is really easier to add the fringe when you have completed the rug. Hook it as already described, turning in the rough ends and working a plaited stitch edging up the sides as you go. For the fringe prepare lengths of cotton thread according to the width of fringe you want, remembering that the threads will be only half as long when they are knotted in the fringe.

Place the rug across a table and secure it with a weight. Then facing the shorter side of the rug, work from left to right using a latchet hook. Insert the hook under the first canvas thread. Loop the group of cotton threads around the hook holding the ends between your thumb and index finger of the left hand as for the four-movement hooking method.

Pull the hook back under the horizontal thread and then, pushing it forward through the loop, catch the ends in the latchet and bring them back to form a knot. Pull tight to secure.

When you have finished one end of the rug, brush the ends toward you and trim any longer threads to make it even. Steam the fringe to straighten it.

Braids and Arabesques

Here are some exciting braids which are simple to make (see techniques in Macramé chapters 1 and 2, pages 134 and 154). The richness of the final effect comes from the clever use of color. You'll find these braids and arabesques useful for decoration and, in particular, they will give your clothes a really distinctive finishing touch for collars and cuffs, or as most unusual lacy trimming down the front of a dress.

Damascus braid

This braid is made up of half hitches, square knots and blackberry-shaped balls.

To make a ball

Work six square knots, then using a tapestry needle, thread the two central threads from front to back through the work above the center of the first knot. Pull up until a little blackberry-shaped roll is formed. The next knot you work will hold the ball in place.

To start the braid

Set on 16 double threads (on a foundation cord) as follows: 2 blue, 4 pink, 4 blue, 4 pink, 2 blue. Work 1 row of horizontal double half hitches. Then working on the first 4 (blue) threads, make a ball.

Using the next 8 (pink) threads, make a square knot. With the next 8 (blue) make 3 balls using the middle 4 threads for the center ball. Make another square knot with the next 8 (pink) threads, finishing off with 1 ball on the remaining 4 (blue) threads.

▲ *Damascus braid—square knots, half hitch, blackberry-shaped balls*

Under the single balls work 2 double half hitches with the 1st thread over the 2nd and the 4th over the 3rd.

Under the group of 3 balls work 2 double half hitches with the 1st thread over the 2nd and the 8th over the 7th. Then work 2 double half hitches with the 3rd thread over the 4th and the 6th over the 5th.

To bring the blue threads under the pink and vice-versa, use the blue threads as leaders and work 2 rows of diagonal double half hitches, breaking the pattern with a double half hitch on the pair of blue threads. Knot the pink threads which are left hanging, then work 2 more rows of diagonal double half hitch, breaking the

pattern as before by once again working a double half hitch.

To continue, work 4 rows of horizontal double half hitch with the pink threads on each side (each time using the outside pink thread as leader); groups of 4 balls with the blue threads and a square knot with the central pink threads.

Repeat the diagonal double half hitch to reverse the order of the colors and continue to the length required, finishing with a row of horizontal double half hitch. If you prefer, you can finish with a row of knots and leave a fringe.

Alexandria braid

This braid is made up of a combination of square knots and half hitch. Set on 24 double threads as follows: 2 turquoise, 4 saffron, 4 turquoise, 4 saffron, 4 turquoise, 4 saffron, 2 turquoise. Work 2 rows of horizontal double half hitch.

On the first 4 (turquoise) threads work 2 square knots.

With all the groups of saffron threads work a diagonal double half hitch motif crossing in the center as shown in Macramé chapter 1, finishing with a half hitch using the inside pairs of threads. With the groups of 8 (turquoise) threads work clusters of square knots as follows: Work 2 knots with the middle 4 threads, then divide the threads and work 2 knots on each group of 4 threads, finishing with 2 knots using the middle 4 threads again.

To reverse the order of the colors, use the saffron threads as leaders and work 4 rows of diagonal double half hitch, finishing with a half hitch on the first 2 leaders.

Repeat this sequence as many times as you want, always working square knots with the turquoise threads and the diagonal double half hitch motif with the saffron. (On each side of the braid instead of crossing in the center, work diagonal double half hitch back toward the braid using the same leaders.) Finish the braid with 2 rows of horizontal double half hitch.

▼ *Alexandria braid — a combination of square knots and half hitch and a strikingly effective use of color.*

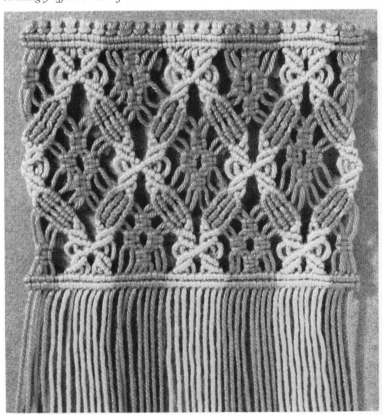

Banister twist

Set on as many threads as you need in multiples of four. Now work 1 row of horizontal double half hitches.

Work as follows on each group of 4 threads:

Using the first left-hand thread as leader, make 1 double half hitch on the 2nd thread.

Using the 4th thread as leader, double half hitch diagonally to the left.

Then using a pin to keep the thread in place, use the same leader to work 1 double half hitch to the right. Now hold the 3rd thread sloping to the right and double half hitch the 4th thread onto it. Pin in place. Now twist this 3rd thread back to act as the leader and double half hitch diagonally from right.

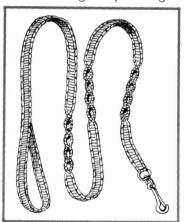

Banister arabesque

This arabesque is based on banister twist and worked as follows:

Set on alternating pairs of ivory and blue double threads.

On the first 4 (ivory) threads work 2 diagonal bars of double half hitch sloping to the left. Work twist motif and then 2 more bars to the left.

Repeat on each group of ivory and blue threads to end of row. Join the pair of threads with 2 bars of diagonal double half hitch so that the colors are reversed. Continue working the above steps alternating the colors with each sequence.

Finish making the banister arabesque with a row of horizontal double half hitch.

▲ *Banister twist with bars sloping to the left*
◀ *Dog leash in banister twists and square knots*

▲ *Banister twist with bars sloping to the right*
▼ *Banister arabesque in two colors*

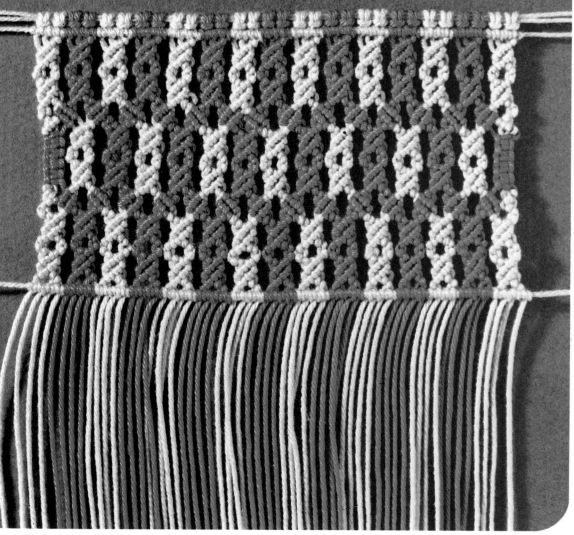

Dress-making 9

Begin with the basic dress

It is every would-be dressmaker's ambition to make a dress successfully, but many give up in despair. They buy a paper pattern, cut out the fabric and plunge in and stitch it together without marking the pattern detail, basting the seams, or trying on the garment for fitting.

Halfway through they find that the garment does not fit, and since they haven't transferred the pattern detail to the fabric, there are no guide lines for altering the dress. Often the result is that the garment is thrown into the back of a drawer and forgotten. With more careful initial preparation, there would be no cause for discouragement and it would be a relatively simple matter to put things right.

Creative Hands has designed a basic dress as part of the special Pattern Pack with both the beginner and the accomplished dressmaker in mind. If you are a beginner, you will find that all the stages of making a dress and detailed fitting instructions are given and also that the pattern pieces are kept to the minimum needed to assemble a dress. Every piece is clearly marked and easy to identify. And, to prevent confusion at the cutting out stages, only the main pattern pieces are cut at first; the facings are cut as you need them.

Watch out for tips for the experienced dressmaker, too. The method used for finishing the inside of the basic dress, the neckline, armholes and center front fastening is the one used by experts to limit bulk on these edges, especially when thick and weighty fabrics are being used. Other finishes are covered in later chapters.

Since assembling the basic dress is clearly explained step by step, when you come to other dresses you will be able to refer to the techniques for putting on tab front fastenings, finishing and fitting contained in these chapters.

The basic dress

This is where we introduce the Pattern Pack given in Volume 22. The first garment from the Pack is the basic dress, shown here in blue wool. The pattern is so versatile that you can make a whole wardrobe of dresses based on this one pattern. Being semi-tailored the style lends itself to a wide variety of fabrics, the mood of the dress depending on the fabric and trimming used.

Here are a few suggestions: For a sporty version, use a crisp fabric and top stitch the collar and tab details; for parties use voile or silk; for more formal occasions extend the pattern to full length and make an evening dress in a glamorous printed silk.

Later chapters explain in detail how to use the basic dress to make the other styles sketched here, which are only a few from the complete Creative Hands wardrobe of styles to make. However, for those of you who are advanced dressmakers, having the Pattern Pack enables you to make any one of these versions of the basic dress right away.

◄ *The basic dress, without sleeves*
▼ *Four versions of the basic style*

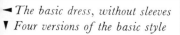

Tunic style

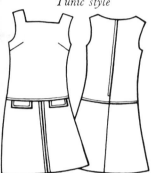

Jumper style

Shirtwaist style

Long evening dress
Midi version with fitted sleeves ►

Choosing your fabric

If you're a beginner, use a firmly woven fabric which does not fray easily, such as wool flannel, fine tweed or a worsted woolen fabric. All these are easy to handle, retain their shape and will not slip around during making.

Here is a list of other fabrics which are also suitable for the basic dress.

- ☐ **Firmly woven cottons:** Sailcloth, dress-weight poplin, lightweight denim and piqué.
- ☐ **Linens:** Dress-weight, plain or embroidered.
- ☐ **Man-made fabrics:** Cloth made from, or containing, acrylic or polyester fiber, such as Acrilan or Dacron.
- ☐ **Wool or wool mixtures:** Viyella, wool crepe and many traditional woolen dress-weight fabrics.

And here are some more fabrics which require a little more dressmaking know-how.

- ☐ **Silks, pure and synthetic:** Shantung, Honan and Thai silk, foulard and brocade.
- ☐ **Cotton:** Organdy and voile.

The basic dress can also be made from jersey fabric, with the exception of the silk or silk-type jerseys. Before buying jersey, test it by holding it up over your wrist. If there is a downward drag to the fabric—almost as though it is weighted—it is more suitable for softly draped styles and not for the semi-tailored style of the basic dress.

Fabric requirements and notions

Before buying the dress and facing fabric, look at the yardages given on the pattern sheet. To face the woolen and silk fabrics, use pure silk or rayon taffeta. Avoid triacetates or nylon, because they will not stand as much pressing as is necessary on wool. For cotton and linen use poplin for facing. Man-made fiber fabrics should be finished with fabric of equal weight, strength and texture. If your dress is washable, remember to buy washable facing fabric. You will also need the following notions: 8 buttons; 9 sew-on snaps size 0; matching thread.

Sewing psychology

Dressmaking needs careful planning. In order to be successful, each job must follow the preceding one in natural and logical succession. Never let each step of the work become an end in itself, but let it be a means to an end.

Making a basic skirt is a simple task, but with a dress the detail increases. It takes more time to make and real planning is essential. It can be a great temptation to rush ahead and do things out of order because you are impatient to see the finished result, but unless you are methodical you can easily ruin the garment.

When you've pinned the paper pattern onto the fabric, and cut the dress, tailor's tack all the details, bearing in mind that this will help you with the next step. The next three stages are the most important ones: basting the seams together, fitting the dress, and making the fitting alterations before sewing up the seams. If you neglect these preliminaries, you can find yourself with an ill-fitting garment when it's too late to alter it.

So, plan your dressmaking. Always remember to concentrate on doing the job in hand so that you can do the next one properly.

In this way you will enjoy your work and the results will be good. It is also worth the extra time to read through the whole of each chapter before taking action, because this will help your planning and avoid possible disaster later on.

Reading the Creative Hands Pattern Pack pieces

Before cutting out any pattern, take a moment to look at it so that you can identify the paper pattern pieces and get to know what the markings mean. Take the dress pattern and lay it on a table in front of you. You may find it easier to study the pattern pieces on the opposite page.

The four pattern pieces needed for the basic dress are the back, front, tab and collar patterns. Note the seamlines: The pattern does not give seam allowances, so the solid lines are also stitching lines. Look at the balance marks, which will have to be matched. For instance, the balance mark on the side seam of the dress back meets the end of the side bust dart on the dress front. The shoulder balance marks on back and front will have to meet when stitching the shoulder seams.

Next, look at the dotted lines, which indicate stitching lines and optional darts. The dart shown on the shoulder of the dress back is optional, as some fabrics will ease in between the balance marks; but if you need more fullness across the back shoulder line, or if your fabric is too stiff to ease in, then you will need this dart for a smooth fitting shoulder line.

The long body darts are also optional and largely a matter of style and fashion, except in the case of larger bust sizes, when they become a must.

The long, pointed dotted line parallel to the center front is the stitching line for the tab on the right front and the meeting line for the tab on the left front, when the tab is wrapped over for fastening.

The two solid horizontal lines across the back and front are for lengthening or shortening the pattern. The dotted line on the tab pattern is the center front, and the dotted lines below the solid line of the lower armhole are stitching lines used when making the dress with sleeves.

Cutting out the paper pattern

Cut out the back, collar and tab paper pattern pieces along the solid outlines. Then cut out the front, leaving a ½in margin along the shoulder and side seams, outside the solid pattern outline. Do not cut out the side bust dart, however (see the upper diagram on page 179).

Correcting the pattern length

As the pattern has been made with neither seam nor hem allowances, it is easy to check the final length as follows:

Pleat the pattern at the side bust dart by placing the lower seamline at the upper seamline, and securing it with pins.

Lap the back shoulder seam over the margin on the front shoulder seam to meet the solid seamlines, and pin. Join the side seam in the same way.

Slip the pattern over your shoulder and stand sideways in front of a long mirror so that you can see the final length of your dress. If you need more or less length, measure the amount you need, take off the dress and unpin it. Then make the length adjustments along the two solid horizontal lines.

The dress length given comes to just below the knee for a 5ft 5in height. If you are taller or shorter and want to alter the dress to obtain this length, use the two solid lines as described below. If, however, you simply want the dress to be longer, you can add up to 5in by using the two solid lines across the skirt of the dress. If this is not enough and you need still more length, just add that to the hemline.

To lengthen the pattern, cut the pattern along the solid horizontal lines and fix strips of paper between the pattern sections to make up the required length.

To shorten the pattern, simply make a pleat along each horizontal line, to the depth of the required amount.

Re-pin the darts and the shoulder and side seams and slip the pattern on once again for a final check to see that you have made the right adjustments.

Take out all the pins and cut off the margins on the dress front. Also cut into the underarm bust darts.

Preparing the fabric for cutting

Prepare the fabric in the same way as for the basic skirt in Dressmaking chapter 5, page 96. Smooth out any creases with a warm iron and a damp or dry cloth, according to the fabric type.

When working on longer lengths of fabric, it becomes difficult to find a surface large enough to accommodate the full length, so use a chair back to support the rest of the fabric. This prevents any pull on the fabric on which you are working.

Check that the selvages of the fabric are not tight and making the fabric pucker. If they are, make small snips through the selvages only, about 2in apart. If this doesn't make the fabric lie flat, cut off the selvages altogether.

Select the appropriate layout from the special sheet and follow it carefully.

Leave enough room between pattern pieces for ¾in seam and 2½in hem allowances. Pin down your pattern pieces securely.

Beware—before you cut

Having studied figure types and problems in Dressmaking chapter 3, page 54, you may have discovered that you need to make certain adjustments to your pattern before cutting out. Later chapters deal fully with pattern adjustments, but because of the soft fit of the basic dress, figure problems are quite easily overcome, provided you take the following precautions.

Straight shoulders. For very straight shoulders, add ½in to the normal seam allowance toward the outer edge of the shoulder seam, as you may have to let it out.

Rounded back and sloping shoulders. For a slightly rounded back and sloping shoulders, leave an extra deep seam allowance along the back armhole edge, about 1½in at shoulder level, tapering into normal seam allowance toward the underarm.

Thick-set neck. If you have a thick-set neck, measure your neck around the base, then measure the neck edge of the center back to center front of the pattern. This measurement should be 1in larger than your own. If it is not, do not cut the collar until you have fitted the dress.

Large proportions. It is always a good idea to leave an extra seam allowance where you know your measurements are slightly larger than standard proportions. You can then make the necessary adjustments when you are fitting the garment.

Pinning the hem and seam allowances

Mark the hem and seam allowances with pins or tailor's chalk. Pin ¾in seam and 2½in hem allowances all around, and if you need to make any of the alterations mentioned above, add the additional allowances now.

Add the extra seam allowance at the darts as shown in the top right-hand diagram.

You will notice the layout on the special sheet in the Pack shows extra width on the center front seams. This is a double seam allowance of 1½in and you will see how to use this later. Leave on this double seam allowance when you cut out.

You are now ready to cut out the fabric. The pattern details will be marked after cutting.

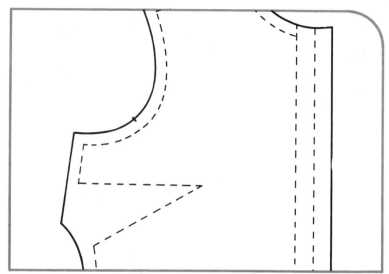

▲ *Add seam allowance at the darts* ▼ *Basic dress pattern pieces*

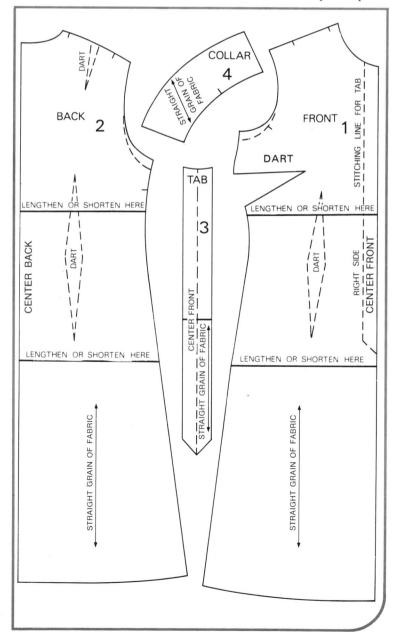

179

Fashion Flair
Braiding & cord work

Use cord and braid to give a mass-produced paper pattern garment or last year's plain dress interesting design detailing.

If you make a garment in a reversible fabric, you can finish off the raw edges with fold-over braid. Cut off seam allowances, then stay stitch edge with a machine stitch a little less than half the width of the braid from edge.

Lay raw edge of fabric into fold of braid.

Pin, baste and stitch, checking that the edges of the braid on the top side and underneath are even.

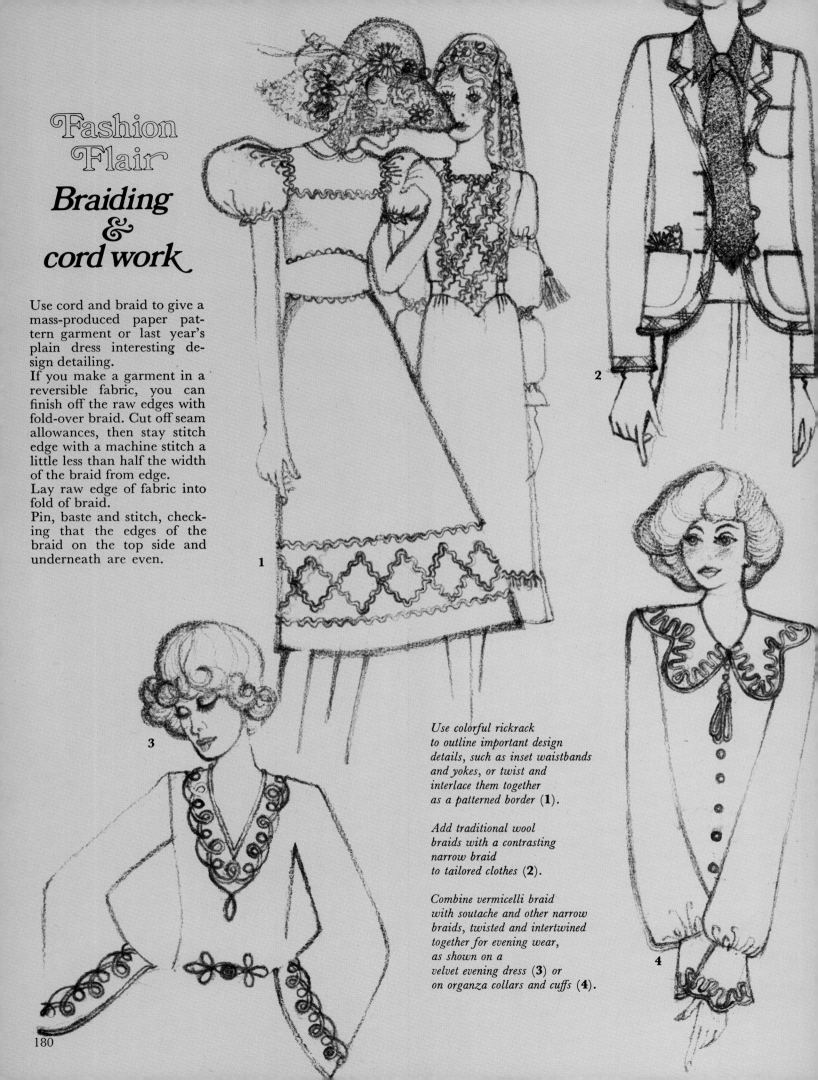

Use colorful rickrack to outline important design details, such as inset waistbands and yokes, or twist and interlace them together as a patterned border (**1**).

Add traditional wool braids with a contrasting narrow braid to tailored clothes (**2**).

Combine vermicelli braid with soutache and other narrow braids, twisted and intertwined together for evening wear, as shown on a velvet evening dress (**3**) or on organza collars and cuffs (**4**).

Bulgarian embroidery

This rich design is of Bulgarian peasant origin and embroidered in slanting Slav stitch, worked across two threads and up four on an even-weave fabric. The black outline stitch is backstitch and the tiny squares are filled with four cross-stitches. The richness in color and boldness of the design suggest a dramatic wall panel. Or, a single motif would look striking on a cushion.

Worked on an even-weave linen with 21 threads to the inch, the motif measures about 9½in by 10in. The design is embroidered in DMC 6-strand floss (3 strands used throughout) with pearl cotton for the highlight areas. The 6-strand floss colors are: red, tangerine, black and in pearl cotton size 5: geranium, blue, pale green, gold, yellow, cream, and turquoise. The combination of bright colors gives the design its peasant look.

Pattern Library

The secret of knitting success

Knitting Know-how 10

Your finished garment can and should look just as attractive and well-fitting as it does in the photograph which catches your eye. The secret of knitting success lies in remembering to read through all the directions before you even consider putting needles to yarn. Otherwise it is all too easy to end up with a garment which is so small that you can't squeeze into it or so enormous that you have room to spare. Don't allow yourself to be carried away by that first rush of enthusiasm to cast on and start knitting. Make sure before you start that you completely understand everything, from buying the yarn to the final pressing. Publication styles vary, but basically directions fall into three sections:
1. Materials required and finished sizes
2. Working directions
3. Finishing details
The first section is often the most neglected, but all three are of vital importance to the success of your garment.

Sizes

Check that the pattern actually provides you with the size you want. If it is one size smaller or larger than required, the results will be unsatisfactory. If the skirt or sleeve length needs alteration, read through the working instructions to see if the design allows for this adjustment. It is usually only where a large, intricate repeat is used that alterations in length may be difficult.

After the actual measurements of the design are stated, you will generally find that the smallest size is given first throughout the directions. Any alterations for other sizes follow in order in either square brackets [] or parentheses (). If you find that only one figure is given, then you can be sure that this applies to all sizes.

Gauge

Although it is often ignored completely, the section on gauge is the key to your success. If you don't get the same number of stitches and rows to the inch as the designer, then no amount of careful knitting and finishing will give you a perfect garment.

To obtain the correct gauge, you may have to change the size needles that you use. If you have too many stitches to the inch, you will need to try a size larger pair of needles. If you have too few stitches to the inch, you will need to use a size smaller pair. (The fact that you may have to use a different needle size is of no importance at all. What is of the greatest importance is that you obtain the same number of stitches and rows as the designer.) When knitting a gauge square, never try to measure over only one inch. It is much easier to measure over not less than 4 inches. If there is even a quarter of a stitch too many or too few, it will begin to show over 4 inches, whereas over an inch it is too easy to feel that it is not enough of a difference to matter. Measure on a flat surface and don't be tempted to pull the sample to the right size!

Ignoring notes on gauge or yarn may lead to garments like these!

Materials

Some designs have been worked out for the knitting yarn which is stated; therefore, you should try to use this brand if you want your garment to look like the picture. If for any reason it is just impossible for you to obtain the recommended yarn, then you can substitute something else. But again, you must make absolutely sure that you can achieve the gauge stated. Even if the pattern just calls for a simple knitting worsted, don't assume that every other knitting worsted yarn will automatically knit up to the same gauge. You can only be certain by working sample squares until you find a yarn which works up identically.

If you use a different yarn from the brand given, you may find that you have to use a slightly different quantity. The quantity given only applies to the stated brand.

Always buy or reserve enough yarn to complete the garment. If you fail to do this, you may have to buy extra balls of a different dye lot. This means that it will be the same yarn, but it will have been dyed at a different time. The color can vary enough to cause an unsightly stripe across your work where the two different dyes meet. Each ball of yarn is marked not only with the shade number but also with a dye lot number, so you can always tell whether or not all the balls are the same.

Do not overlook the fact that needles and stitch holders should be in good condition. Bent, twisted or roughened needles or holders will spoil the yarn and make the best knitting irregular. If it has been many years since you bought new needles, perhaps now is the time to treat yourself to some new tools.

Measuring knitting

When measuring knitting, lay it on a flat surface. It is very tempting to try to measure with your work lying along your knee or on the arm of your chair, but you must be accurate and not just hope that it is correct. Always measure with a rigid ruler, not a tape, and don't be tempted to stretch it 'just a little' so that you can avoid having to work those extra few rows before reaching the next stage. It will really take you longer if you do this, because you will find that the sections don't fit together when you try to finish the garment. Also, never measure around a curve. If you want to measure an armhole, then you must measure the depth on a straight line. In the same way, to measure a sleeve don't measure up the sloping side, but up the center of the work.

Points to note

The main sections of a garment are usually given first in the directions (although sometimes a small section such as a pocket lining must be worked before beginning the main section, so that it is ready to join in when required). Where an asterisk* occurs, it means repeat and is used in two different ways. It may appear in the directions for one particular row, where it means repeat from that point as directed. Or you may find it before the beginning of a sentence, and sometimes after a paragraph, to show a part which is repeated later in the directions. The section(s) to be repeated will always be made clear.

In some designs, the rows which form the pattern to be repeated throughout the garment are given in a note on their own before the directions begin. If you read through the directions before starting, you will spot these notes and know to refer back to them when you read 'continue in pattern'.

Where there is only brief mention about casting on and binding off or increasing and decreasing, you may find it helpful to look back to the specific chapters for details on these points.

Marker threads

Occasionally you are directed in a design to place a marker thread at one or both ends of a row. This acts as a visual guide so that this point can be identified easily later in the directions, either as a point for measuring to or from, or in order to assist when it comes to finishing. All that is required is that a short length of any contrasting yarn is threaded through the stitch and tied in place so that it does not accidentally come out while you are working. It is always removed after it has served its purpose.

Finishing

Details are always given in the order in which the sections are to be assembled along with directions for edges and finishing. Also in this part of the instructions you will find a guide to whether or not you should press the yarn. Again, remember that the directions refer to the most suitable yarn for the particular pattern. It is most important to ascertain whether or not the yarn can stand pressing. Some man-made fibers can be completely spoiled by pressing and it would be too bad to ruin your garment.

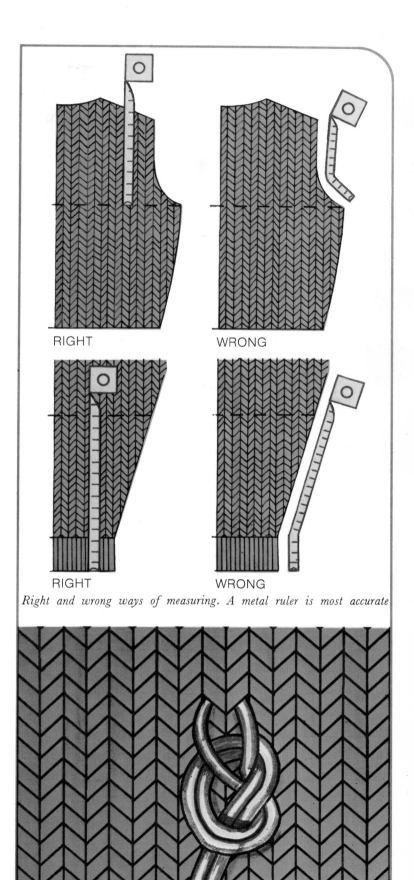

RIGHT   WRONG

RIGHT   WRONG

Right and wrong ways of measuring. A metal ruler is most accurate

The marker thread

Collector's Piece

Painting with yarn

This beautiful sleeveless jacket is—
believe it or not—hand knitted! Since
it is the instinctive design of an
experienced knitter, it is easily comparable
to an original, one-of-a-kind painting:
Reproductions are not available and,
regrettably, explicit directions do not
exist. For those who want to try to
emulate it, the general technique is all
that can be explained.

Every patch of color is knitted at random
and every shape is different from the
rest. Some patches are worked in
stockinette stitch, others in seed stitch,
broken rib or garter stitch. Even
the yarns are mixed to include smooth
and textured ones, with a few patches
of mohair or angora.

The designer worked on the principle of
first planning the outline shape of the
garment. She next chose the colors and
yarns and decided on the general
outline of the pattern shapes—here they
are irregular and angular, but they
could be curved or geometric. Then,
having cast on the number of stitches
needed for the particular garment,
the knitter made the hem in one color
and then started working, say, 12 stitches
of one color, 10 stitches of the next
color in maybe a different wool, 15
stitches of the next and so on. The knitter sat
surrounded by separate balls of the yarns
in the colors selected—she didn't
carry the strands across the inside of the
work as in Fair Isle. If you look carefully,
you will see that at least a dozen
different balls of yarn were used
across the back of this jerkin, but no one
ball was worked twice in a single row. The
knitter worked out the color and stitch
patterns as she went along, being careful
to follow the shaping. As one
color was finished and the next intro-
duced, the yarn was broken off.

The secret of the astonishingly tidy
inside of the jerkin is that every tail
was darned in meticulously along the
color seamlines.

If you do try this method, keep in mind
one vital point: Always use wools that knit
up to the same gauge, otherwise your fabric
will pucker. But if you can't resist
including a yarn with a slightly different
gauge, change onto a sock needle for
the patch (as for cabling) while working
this area so that you achieve the same
number of stitches to the inch.

Knit him a casual sweater

No man can have too many sweaters! This casual style, with its round neck, set-in sleeves and stripes in a different color, looks good and is easy to knit.

Sizes
Directions are for 38in chest. Length down center back, 27½ [27¾:28:28¼]in. Sleeve seam from wrist to underarm, 20½ [21:21¼:21½]in, adjustable.
The figures in brackets [] refer to the 40, 42 and 44in sizes respectively.

Gauge
6 sts and 8 rows to 1in over stockinette st, worked on No.5 needles

Materials
Sports yarn 5 [6:6:7] 2oz balls in main color
1 ball in contrast
One pair No. 3 needles or Canadian No. 10
One pair No. 5 needles or Canadian No. 8
One cable needle
Two stitch holders

Back

Using No.3 needles and main color, cast on 128 [136:144:152] sts.
* * **1st row** * K2, P2, rep from * to end.
Continue in ribbing, working 9 rows more in main color.
Work 4 rows contrast, 2 rows main color, 4 rows contrast and 10 rows main color, inc one st at beg of last row. **
129 [137:145:153] sts.

186

Change to No.5 needles and cable pattern as follows:
1st row K8 [12:16:20], P2, K7, * P2, K6, P2, K7, rep from * to last 10 [14:18:22] sts, P2, K8 [12:16:20].
2nd row P8 [12:16:20], K2, P7, * K2, P6, K2, P7, rep from * to last 10 [14:18:22] sts, K2, P8 [12:16:20].
Rep 1st and 2nd rows 8 times more.
19th row K8 [12:16:20], P2, K7, * P2, slip next 3sts onto cable needle and hold in back of work, K3, K3 from cable needle—called C6—P2, K7, rep from * to last 10 [14:18:22] sts, P2, K8 [12:16:20].
20th row As 2nd.
These 20 rows form the pattern and are rep throughout, increased sts being worked into stockinette st side panels as they are made.
Continue in patt, inc one st at each end of next and every 20th row until there are 139 [147:155:163] sts.
Work without further shaping until 19in, or desired length to underarm, ending with a WS row.

Shape armholes
Bind off 3 [4:5:6] sts at beg of next 2 rows.
Dec one st at each end every other row 10 [11:12:13] times.
113 [117:121:125] sts.
Work 43 rows more in patt.

Shape shoulders
Bind off 12 [13:14:15] sts at beg of next 2 rows.
Bind off 12sts at beg of next 4 rows.
Slip rem sts on holder.

Front

Work as given for back until 21 rows have been worked after armhole shaping, ending with a WS row.

Shape neck
1st row Patt 46 [47:48:49], turn. Complete left shoulder on these sts.
***Dec one st at neck edge on next 6 rows, then on every RS row until 36 [37:38:39] sts rem.
Work until armhole measures same as back to shoulder, ending at armhole edge.

Shape shoulder
1st row Bind off 12 [13:14:15] sts, patt to end.
Work 1 row.
3rd row Bind off 12sts, patt to end.
Work 1 row.
Bind off rem 12sts. ***
With RS work facing, slip center 21 [23:25:27] sts onto holder and work to end of row.
Complete as for left shoulder, working from *** to ***

Sleeves

Using No.3 needles and main color, cast on 64 [68:72:76] sts.
Work as given for back from ** to **, dec one st at end of last row. 63 [67:71:75] sts.
Change to No.5 needles and continue in patt as follows:
1st row K1 [3:5:7], P2, K6, P2, *K7, P2, K6, P2, rep from * to last 1 [3:5:7] sts, K1 [3:5:7].
2nd row P1 [3:5:7], K2, P6, K2, *P7, K2, P6, K2, rep from * to last 1 [3:5:7] sts, P1 [3:5:7].
Rep 1st and 2nd rows 8 times more.
19th row K1 [3:5:7], P2, C6, P2, *K7, P2, C6, P2, rep from * to last 1 [3:5:7] sts, K1 [3:5:7].
20th row As 2nd.
These 20 rows form the patt and are rep throughout sleeves, inc sts being worked into the patt as they are made.
Continue in patt, inc one st at each end of next and every 6th row until there are 101 [105:109:113] sts.

Work without shaping until sleeve measures 20½in, or desired length, ending with a WS row.

Shape cap
Bind off 3 [4:5:6] sts at beg of next 2 rows.
Dec one st at each end of next and every other row until 77 sts rem.
Bind off.

Neckband

Sew left shoulder-seam.
With RS work facing, No.3 needles and main color, K41 [43:45:47] sts from back holder, pick up and K30 sts down left side of neck, K21 [23:25:27] sts from front holder and pick up and K30 sts up right side of neck.
Work in K2, P2 rib.
Work 3 rows main color, 4 rows contrast, and 18 rows main color.
Bind off in rib.

▲ *Detail of the cable and rib*
Man's striped and cabled sweater ▶

Finishing

Press all pieces lightly, under a damp cloth with a warm iron, avoiding ribbed edges.
Sew right shoulder and neckband.
Sew side and sleeve seams.
Set in sleeves.
Fold neckband in half to WS and sl st loosely in place.

Trimmings and borders galore

Lace picot

Ch2, * into the first of these 2ch insert the hook, yoh, and draw through one loop. There are now 2 loops on hook (top photograph). Into the loop nearest the hook point ch2. Slip both loops off hook and insert hook back into only the loop farther to the left (bottom photograph). Without turning the work, rep from * until the edging is the desired length. Finish off.

Some of the most attractive crochet edgings are worked from variations of picot stitches. They can be made in thick yarns to give a chunky edge or in the finest cotton for a delicate cobweb effect. The border can be made to the desired length and then sewed in place, or worked directly onto the garment if the edge to be trimmed is knitted or of a loose enough weave to allow a crochet hook to be inserted easily. Don't stop at a single basic edging. Try a second line overlapping the first or sew on row after row to give a soft layered effect like a many-petaled flower.

Lace picot: ▲ *two loops on hook and* ▼ *hook back in one loop only*

Small picot edging

* Ch3, work 2sc into the first of these 3ch. Without turning the work rep from * until the strip is the required length. Finish off. If this edging is to be worked directly onto the edge to be trimmed (as in the bottom photograph), begin by working 1sc into the fabric, * ch3, work 2sc into the first of the 3ch, skip a small section of edge of fabric and work 1sc into fabric. Continue in this way from * until all the edge has been worked. When working an edging all around a square or circular shape, finish at the point where you started, and join to the first stitch with a slip stitch.

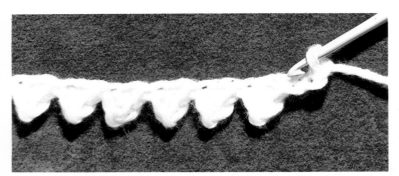

Small picot edging: ▲ *worked separately and* ▼ *worked directly onto cloth*

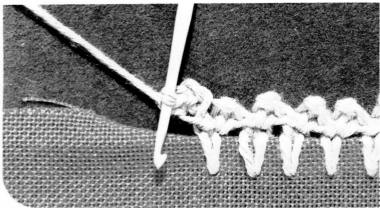

A collection of ideas to get you experimenting with crochet picot edgings — they can be worked to match or contrast to provide a pretty finishing touch.

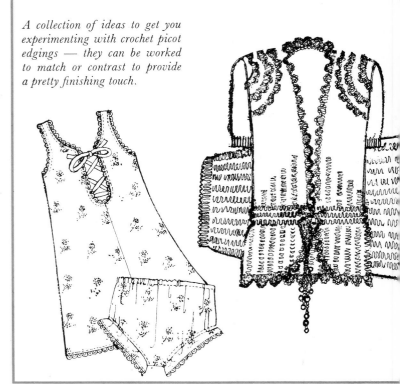

Ring picot

* Ch5, work 1 dc into the first of these 5ch. Without turning the work, rep from * until the edging is the desired length. Finish off.

Leaf picot

* Ch3, work 3dc into the first of these 3ch. Do not turn the work but rep from * until the edging is the desired length. Finish off.

Rounded picot

* Ch3, work 1 sc into the first of these 3ch. Do not turn the work but rep from * until the edging is the desired length. Finish off.

Pointed picot

* Ch5, work 1 ss into 2nd ch from hook, 1 sc into next ch, 1 hdc into next ch, and 1 dc into last ch. Do not turn work but rep from * until the edging is the desired length. Finish off.

N.B. Check back to chapters 1 and 2 for crochet abbreviations.

▲ *Ring picot: shown actual size* ▼ *Leaf picot: close-up detail*

▼ *Pointed picot: distinctive look* *Rounded picot: a narrower effect* ►

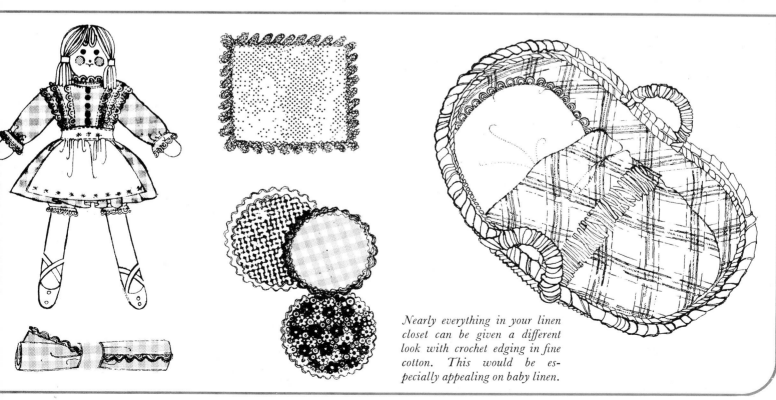

Nearly everything in your linen closet can be given a different look with crochet edging in fine cotton. This would be especially appealing on baby linen.

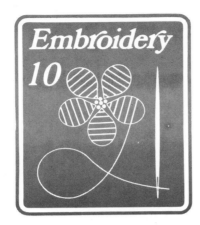

Buttonhole all sorts of edges

Buttonhole stitch has many decorative uses besides the obvious practical one. It is the strongest way of doing appliqué and is also useful for binding raw edges in cutwork and scalloping. Work buttonhole stitch motifs on a blouse, dress or handkerchief case. Each stitch can be threaded, knotted, whipped or worked in groups—there are countless variations to have fun with.

Buttonhole stitch or blanket stitch

Simple buttonhole or blanket stitch is worked from left to right. Bring the needle out on the lower line, then insert the needle above and a little to the right and make a straight downward stitch, pulling the needle through over the working thread. This forms a row of straight stitches with a closely knotted edge on the lower line.

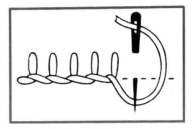

Buttonhole edging

The buttonhole stitch is worked before trimming away the fabric—not the other way around. Cut as close as possible to the edge of the stitching with a small, sharp pair of scissors, being careful not to cut into the stitching itself. The edges should be clean with no fraying visible.

Buttonhole wheel

Arrange the stitches in a circle, taking each stitch into the same central spot so that they pull a hole in the fabric. On closely woven fabrics it is helpful to start the hole with an embroidery stiletto.

Paillettes and mirrors

Add another dimension to buttonhole stitch by fixing mirrors or paillettes onto material. Simply make a circle of buttonhole stitches so that

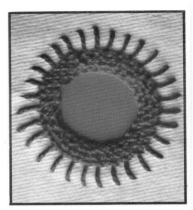

the knots lie toward the center and frame the edge of the paillette. Then work buttonhole stitches into the looped edge of the last row of stitches, building up two or three rows. Always point the needle toward the center and pull the thread tight making a round, looped pocket to hold the mirror or paillette in place.

Closed buttonhole stitch

This is similar to simple buttonhole stitch, with the stitches worked in groups of two or three to form triangles as shown in the diagram.

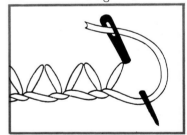

Padded buttonhole stitch

Prepare this in the same way as padded satin stitch. Then, work the buttonhole stitch over the padding. This is especially useful for strengthening any scalloped edges.

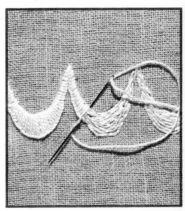

190

Buttonhole stitch ideas

The sketch on the opposite page gives a few ideas for using buttonhole stitch in dress embroidery. As you see, it doesn't take an enormous amount of time and effort to make a plain dress look really pretty. Just embroider some simple motifs on the collar and cuffs, or a pocket or belt, and you've given the dress a fresh look.

Buttonhole a flower motif

Here's a very simple motif to buttonhole. However, if you don't want to do buttonhole stitch, try satin stitch petals with a center of French knots, or outline the flower with French knots and do a satin stitch center.

Handkerchief cases

You can make one of these handkerchief cases in a firm, medium-weight cotton or linen. The edges are scalloped with padded buttonhole stitch, and the flower motifs are delightfully simple.

In fact they are versatile, too, because you can use them in many different ways. Try the violets on a white silk scarf or the flower chain around the yoke of a baby's dress.

To do this, first trace the motifs from the page and transfer them onto the fabric as described in Embroidery chapter 4, page 68. Work the stems in outline stitch, satin stitch the leaves and petals, or try any stitch variation you like. You can either follow the guide to thread and colors used here or choose favorites of your own. Both cases are worked in 6-strand embroidery floss.

For the violet case use grass green for stems and edging, violet for flowers, with touches of orange/red and black.

For the flower chain handkerchief case, the stems and edging are in emerald green, the flowers in pink and bright yellow. Or you could turn them into forget-me-knots with blue petals, or, for that matter, you could work the flowers in any colors you choose.

▲ *Padded buttonhole stitch flowers on a hanky case*   ▼ *Trace this diagram for scalloped edge and motifs*

▲ *Three variations of a simple flower motif*   ▼ *Life-like violets are attractive and easy to work*

Shaggy rug story

Rya means shaggy. Because the density of its pile is good insulation against the cold winters, the rya is found all over Scandinavia. Originally ryas were woven on a loom, but now the pile is knotted on a special backing with a needle. You can, however, use a canvas foundation and knot the wool with a latchet hook. In this way you achieve the shaggy pile and subtle colors of a real rya.

Color blended ryas

Rya rugs have an individual style of coloring. Each knot is made of three strands of yarn which allows enormous scope for using different shades of color to build up a rich texture. A colorful rya rug makes an attractive and very cosy addition to your home whether you use it formally on the floor or hung on the wall. A rya floor cushion is quick to make and, as an introduction to the technique, gives a good idea of the versatility of this method of rug making. The cushion can be made any size—24in square makes a comfortable seat and is not too big to move around easily.

Materials

The canvas to use has 10 squares to 3in and the most suitable yarn is a twisted 2-ply coarse rya yarn which comes in 25 (and 50) gram skeins. Each skein makes approximately 56 (112) knots.

Cutting the skeins

Cut the skeins into pieces the correct length for working. Open out the skein of yarn and, holding it fully extended, cut cleanly through the two ends. Then fold these lengths in half and cut again, halve and cut once more. The skein is now divided into eight and you have a pile of cut threads. (It's a good idea to keep the different colored cut pieces in separate plastic bags.) If the cut lengths seem a bit irregular don't bother to trim them as the general look of the rug is shaggy.

Working a rya

Turn in all raw edges as for the thick pile rugs and start to hook in the tufts from left to right (right to left if you are left-handed) using three strands of yarn in each knot. If you are making a rug, remember to work an edging stitch along one end and partly

up both sides before you start. This isn't necessary for a floor cushion as you will be sewing it to a backing, but leave the first and last threads free along all sides.

With skeins of closely related colors rather than complete contrasts, you can grade the colors as you wish, increasing or decreasing a color to get the required intensity or softness. Hook every alternate row, that is, leave one horizontal thread of canvas free between each row of knots. (If every row were worked, the rug would become terribly heavy.)

Backing a floor cushion

When completed the cushion will need backing with a sturdy upholstery material, as this is the side that will be getting the most wear. Choose a color that blends with the colors you have used for the rya top.

Cut a square of backing material ¾in larger than the size of the worked canvas. Put the two right sides together, pinning them firmly. Sew through from the canvas side, stab stitching through to the backing catching each thread of canvas all around the hooked area. Leave one side open, turn inside out and stuff the cushion firmly with either two old pillows or a 24in cushion pad, available at some upholstery supply houses. Or use kapok or Dacron filling.

5 movement Latchet hook method

The second method for hooking both short pile and rya-type rugs is the 5-movement method. The 4-movement method was shown in Hooked Rugs chapter 1, page 132 where it was explained that using the two methods two people can knot a rug—one at each end—at the same time.

1. Turn up the cut end of the canvas as before and insert the latchet hook under the first of the horizontal (weft) threads.

2. Hold the two ends of the piece of yarn with your left hand and loop it over the hook.

3. Pull the hook back through the canvas until the yarn loop is halfway through the hole, then push the hook through the loop until the latchet is clear.

4. Turn the latchet hook, place the cut ends in the crook and pull the hook back through the loop. The latchet closes automatically.

5. Be sure to pull the knot tight.

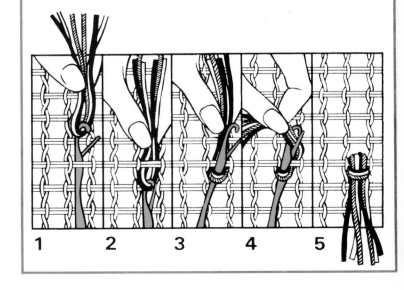

Here's an idea for the nursery—
a large, cuddly porcupine which is
soft enough to sit on. Make him
from burlap, stuff with kapok or
foam, and then sew on a shaggy rya
back. Also shown on this page is a
fine example of a real rya rug.

Fresh as a daisy

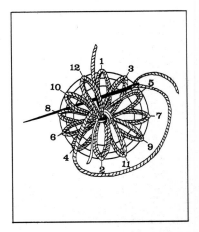

You would be surprised what you can make from a daisy and how easy they are to do! Once you have tried daisy work, you won't be able to put it down—nor will the children. It is so quick you can make dozens of them in an evening while watching television or whiling away a long journey. Two daisies make a pair of earrings, six a headband or choker, twelve add up to a doll's dress, sixteen an unusual belt. And if you keep going, you can soon make enough for a poncho, shawl, or even a long skirt. This chapter covers making separate flowers, while later chapters tell you how to sew and crochet them together and how to fill the center to make very decorative daisies.

Daisies in the making

Daisies can be made from whatever you like, usually wool or thick cotton yarns—or even string, lurex or raffia. Daisies can be washed, but are impossible to iron without flattening. So either choose a bulky man-made yarn which will spring back into shape after washing or be prepared for dry-cleaning.

Most needlework departments stock the Hero Crazy Daisy Winder in 2 inch and 3 inch diameters. To make your own, or to make larger or smaller daisies, simply stick ordinary straight pins around a ring of thick cardboard and pull out the pins when the daisy is completely finished.

Separate daisies

With manufactured daisy makers you will see from the directions that you have to turn the knob to push out the spokes. Hold the daisy maker in the left hand with the flat side facing you. If you are making your own, insert 12 pins around a circle of cardboard 2 inches in diameter.

Hold the end of yarn down with the left thumb. Then, working in a clockwise direction, pass

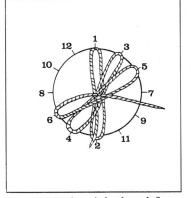

yarn with the right hand from left to right around spoke 1, pass yarn across center and

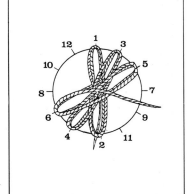

from right to left around spoke 2 opposite, back across center; from left to right around spoke 3, and right to left around spoke 4. Continue until all spokes have been wrapped (once if using thick yarn, several times for thinner yarn) and cut, leaving a tail about 12 inches long.

Closed centers

For a one-color daisy, thread needle with the tail of yarn. Work 13 back stitches, passing needle under 2 petals and back over 1. Make sure to do all 13 back stitches or the center will not be complete. Work in the

starting end with weaving stitches to bind it firmly, and fasten both yarns on the top side of the daisy (this will be the back when the daisy is finished). Pull in the spokes or pull out your pins, and the daisy is complete.

To make a daisy with a center in a contrasting color, take a second yarn, secure it to the center of the daisy with two or three back stitches and continue as before, remembering to bind in both ends of the first color.

Daisy trimmings

Use separate daisies as a trimming — they look so sweet scattered on the little girl's party dress shown opposite. For a twelve year old party-goer, trim the yoke of a plain navy or red dress with white daisies or scatter them around the hem. For a winter bride make a full-length creamy wool dress with long belled sleeves and decorate the sleeves in matching daisies of wool yarn with pearls sewn to the centers.

The basic dress

The next stage of making the dress is to mark the pattern details on the fabric. For the skirt in Dressmaking 5, page 96, these were marked before cutting to prevent the beginner from being confused. In this case, however, it is easier to mark the pattern details once the pieces have been cut out.

Marking the pattern details on the fabric

First mark the details on the dress back. Lay it on a flat surface and mark around the pattern edges with continuous tailor's tacks. Make single tailor's tacks at right angles to the seam edges to indicate the balance marks.

Next, the dash lines. Those on the back indicate optional shoulder and waist darts, and need to be marked only if you are using them. To do so make short slits about 3in apart through the pattern with a needle, along the dash lines. Make single tailor's tacks through each slit, being careful not to stitch into the pattern.

Mark the center back fold line with a row of long basting stitches, as you will need this line to check the hang of the dress.

The dress fronts are marked in two stages. First the general pattern details are marked and then the fastening details.

Mark the center front line from hem to neck.

Make slits through the dash line of the tab stitching line and mark with single tailor's tacks. Mark the corner and point especially carefully, because they have to match the shape of the tab. Similarly mark the waist darts if you are using them.

Tailor's tack around the rest of the pattern and into the darts. Mark the balance marks.

For the second stage the layers must be separated as described for the skirt in Dressmaking chapter 5, page 96, so cut through the tailor's tacks. Lay the right front, right side up, on a flat surface in front of you. Mark the ¾in seam allowance along the center front, from the hem upward to where it meets the stitching line of the tab. Then mark a seam allowance along the tab stitching line and cut off the surplus as shown in the diagram.

With the left dress front in front of you, right side up, look at the diagram carefully. You have already marked the center front line and the meeting line for the tab.

Halve the double seam allowance along the center front and mark the line with long basting stitches. Following the red line on the sketch, cut off the extra seam allowance from the lower edge on the center front, where you don't need it. The extra seam allowance along the upper edge will provide you with enough wrap to fasten the dress.

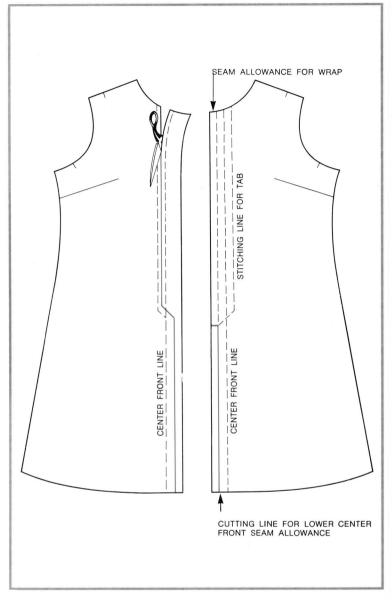

▲ *Preparing the right front*   ▲ *Preparing the left front*

A wrap is usually half the width of the tab (in this pattern, 1 inch) and meets the tab stitching line when closed. But to simplify the cutting of your first dress, only a seam allowance width (¾in) has been given, and this is really plenty. Instructions for cutting a conventional wrap are given later.

On the tab make long basting stitches around the outline and mark the center front line.

Tailor's tack around the collar.

Remove the pattern pieces and separate the layers in the usual way.

Preparing for fitting

The dress is now ready to be pinned and basted to prepare it for fitting.

Pin and baste the darts.

Pin and baste the center front seams from the pointed end of the tab stitching line to the hem.

Pin and baste shoulder and side seams, carefully matching the balance marks.

Press the seams open lightly and turn up the hem.

The fastening detail is not put together at this stage.

Fitting the dress

Before you start fitting, put on the underclothes you will wear with the dress when it is finished. Make sure your bra shoulder straps are adjusted correctly, because if you alter them later your side bust darts will not fit properly.

Slip on the dress and pin the center front opening closed by lapping the raw edge of the seam allowance on the right over the seam allowance for the wrap on the left front.

Now look at the dress in a full length mirror. This is the time when most people wish they'd never started; your dress looks raw and bulky, but don't despair—even experienced dressmakers have to remain very objective at this stage to avoid the feeling.

When fitting, start from the top and work downward. Here is a list of fitting stages in order:

1. The neck
2. The shoulders
3. The armholes
4. The bust
5. The body darts
6. The side seams
7. The hang
8. The length

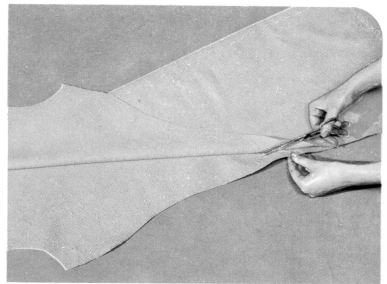
Cutting through the tailor's tacks

1. The neck

Make sure that the row of tailor's tacks around the neck, indicating the stitch line for the collar, lies flat around the base of the neck. If it is strained, or rises on the neck, carefully snip into the seam allowance until you have the required fitting. Do not snip too deeply, because the seam allowance will have to be trimmed and snipped again after you have stitched on the collar. Mark a new stitching line with pins.

2. The shoulders

If the dress lifts at the inner shoulder or feels tight over the top of the arm, it means that your shoulders are straighter than the standard slope of the pattern. Let out a little from the seam allowance on the outer edge of the shoulder line and taper into the original seam allowance toward the neck.

If sloping shoulders make the dress rise at the outer shoulder edges, you will need to lift the seams. Start at the armhole edges and taper into the original seams toward the neck, until the shoulder line lies flat. This may tighten the armholes of the dress. If so, snip the seam allowance carefully where it is tight, until the armholes feel comfortable, and pin new armhole lines.

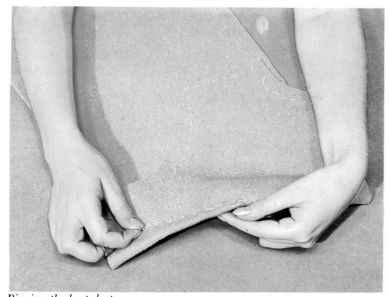
Pinning the bust dart
Pinning the side seams

3. The armholes

If the armholes feel tight and the dress shoulders are caught over the upper arms, your problem is large upper arms.

If the armholes are merely too tight, pin new armhole lines. But if the dress is held away from the neck through tightness around the armholes you must fit this in two stages.

First cut off the seam allowance from the armhole edges around the underarm and slip the dress on again. Then pin new armhole seams. If you have more than the normal seam allowance left outside the new pin lines, take the dress off and pin the armholes together. Mark the pinned armhole line through both layers of fabric and trim to the normal seam allowance. Try on the dress once more to make sure everything is all right.

Finally look at the armhole seamlines over the shoulders and make sure these are in the correct position.

4. The bust

The well-made look of a dress does not depend on your figure, but on the way the dress is fitted to it. So always take the trouble to fit your dress really well, especially over the bustline. The dress should fit smoothly and not strain, even when you are moving. Look at the dart points; these should be in line with the highest point of the bust. If not, pin them higher or lower as required.

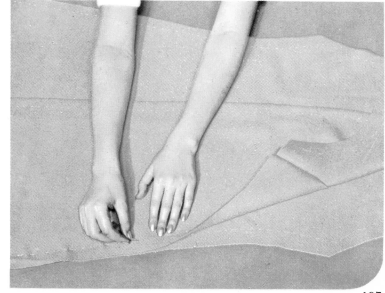

Small adjustments can be made by altering the angle of the darts, but if you have to alter them by more than ½in, it is best to move the whole dart by that amount.

When you have made the necessary adjustments, move around and swing your arms to see how much room you require for movement. Also sit down, as this can tighten the bustline of the dress if you have a large bust.

5. The body darts

If you have used the body darts to make your dress fit more closely, make sure the front darts run toward the bustline and finish just under the highest point of the bust.

The body darts in the back should finish about 2in above the seat. The deepest curve must go through the waistline and not above or below it, as this would leave strain lines.

6. The side seams

Stand sideways in front of a mirror and look at the way the side seams hang. They should run in a straight line all the way down, fitting close to the body at bust level, bypassing the waist and gently flaring toward the hem.

A swing toward the front may be caused by a large bust, which will be dealt with under point 7. If this is not the case and they swing toward the front or back of the dress, it may be that when basting the side seams you eased one side into the other. If so, undo

the side seams and baste them again, making sure that both sides are smooth and flat.

If the dress is too loose, adjust it by pinning the fullness into the side seams.

If your dress is too tight, let out the side seams.

7. The hang

Look at the back of the dress with the help of a hand mirror. The line of basting stitches along the center back line should hang straight. If it is dragged sideways because of tightness, let out the dress at the side seams.

If the basting line hangs toward the right or left, and this is not caused by tightness, you will have to lift the corresponding side seam until the basting line hangs straight. To do this, undo the side seam and lift the dress back into the armhole till the hang is straight. This may leave your armhole too large. If so pin the surplus into the shoulder seam.

The hang of the dress can affect the side seams. A large bust, for instance, will pull the dress up in front, making it jut forward at the hem and pull the side seams toward the front. Undo the side seams and lift more fabric into the underside of the side bust darts. If this gives you too much width in the side seams over the hips, pin extra width into the seam.

A rounded back can cause the same trouble at the back of the dress. To counteract this, undo the side seams and lift the dress

Fitting the dress

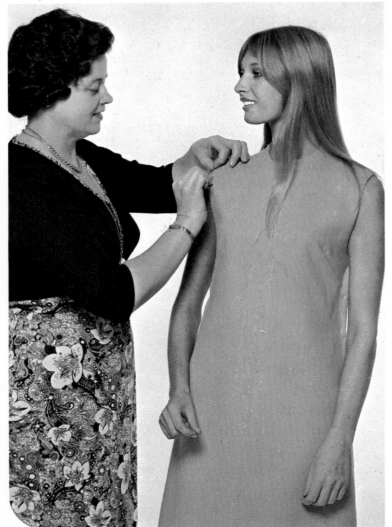

Stitching the dart

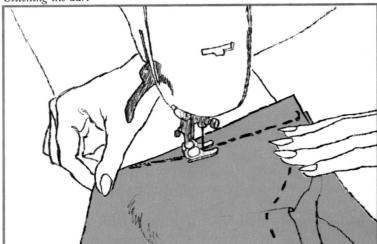

Pressing the dart

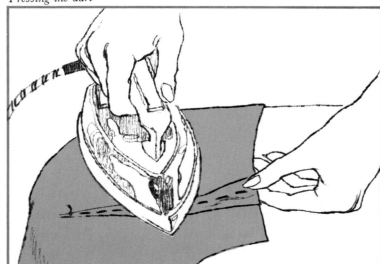

back into the armholes, making sure that you lift it evenly on both sides. Use the balance marks as a guide.

It is difficult to guess the amount to lift, so start by lifting the back by one inch, re-pin the side seams and slip the dress on again. You will then see if the drag toward the underarm has been corrected; if not, lift the dress back a little more.

This adjustment gives you surplus width around the armholes at the back. Lift this surplus into the shoulder seams by first deepening the darts and then making the back shoulder seams slope down a little more, otherwise it will poke out at the armhole points of the shoulder seams.

Line up the armhole seams on the back to the armhole seams on the front, which you will be able to do because you added extra seam allowance when cutting out the fabric.

8. The length

Adjusting the hem is the final stage in the fitting.

If in making your fitting alterations you have adjusted the hang of the dress on one side, level the hemline on that part of the dress with the hemline on the other side.

Marking the corrections

Trace the pin lines, which indicate the new fitting, with basting thread, tracing on each side of the new seamline where the fabric

Pinning the tab to the tab facing

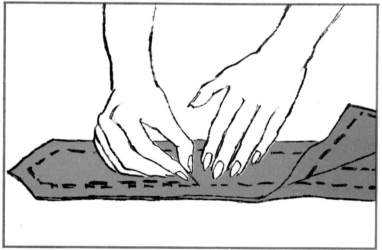

Basting the tab along the stitched edge

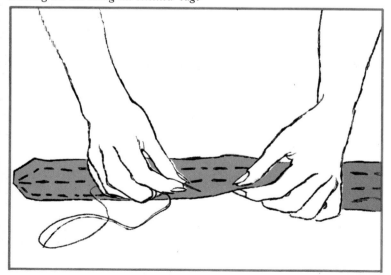

is double, being careful not to catch in both layers at once.

Then remove the pins and basting stitches from these seams. Make sure the fitting corrections are the same on both sides of the dress as shown for the skirt alterations in Dressmaking chapter 6, page 116, unless of course your figure is uneven, when you must fit each side to the shape of your body. Mark the paper pattern pieces too for future reference.

When all the corrections are done, baste the dress together again and make a final fitting.

Stitching

You will be cutting out the under collar and the facings for the center front, tab and armholes as you need them, so have your facing fabric and paper pattern pieces ready.

Test the machine stitches on a scrap of dress material.

To help you plan your work and show you how the stitching and finishing progress, here is a list of the steps involved:

Step 1. The dress front: Darts; center front seam; front fastening, tab and wrap.

Step 2. The dress back: Darts.

Step 3. Joining the dress sections: Shoulder seams; side seams.

Step 4. Finishing the dress: Armholes; collar; hem; finishing the fastening; sew-on snaps; buttons.

Step 1

The dress front. Whenever you have details on a dress such as the center front fastening, it is better to tackle this task before the section you're working on is joined to the remaining sections. This makes for easier handling without the bulk of the dress getting in your way. Undo the basted shoulder and side seams.

Darts. Stitch the side bust darts first. Note that both slanted underarm darts must be sewed in one direction, or else they will twist. This means that one dart will be sewed toward the point and the other toward the base. See in the illustration how the fabric is guided through the machine in the seamline of the dart. Do not pull darts while stitching; they may stretch. After stitching the darts remove the basting and press them flat as you did for the skirt. Pay special attention to the pointed ends. Lay them over the rounded end of the ironing board so that you can mold them into the roundness of the body shape. They must not rise sharply into a point. Molding and shaping the fabric are secrets of good dressmaking. Stitch the waist darts if you are using them. Press them toward the center.

The center front seam. Stitch the center front seam from the pointed end of the tab stitching line to the hem. Remove the basting and press the seam open to within 2in of the upper end.

Front fastening, tab. The first stage is the preparation of the tab. Using the tab pattern, cut out the tab facing from lining fabric with $\frac{3}{4}$in seam allowance all around. Mark the tab pattern details onto the fabric with long basting stitches and make single tailor's tacks through the slits along the dash line.

Pin and baste the tab to the facing with right sides together and with the facing uppermost. Starting at the center front, stitch along the top, down the right side, turn and stitch to the point. Fasten off the stitches securely at both ends so that as you work on the tab the seamlines remain secure.

Trim the seam allowance and clip into the seam at the beginning of the stitching line (center front). Turn the tab to the right side and baste firmly along the sewed edge with small stitches, rolling the facing slightly under to prevent it from showing.

Press this edge carefully on the wrong side of the tab, making sure that the basting stitches do not leave impressions on the fabric, as they will be very difficult to remove.

Directions for finishing the basic dress are given on page 216.

Fashion Flair

Living with the longer look

For a slimmer, more elegant you, try the longer look. Choose midi length for day wear, or full length for a glamorous evening dress. The look encompasses higher, trimmer waists, shorter jackets, and neater heads. Wear it with boots or high vamped shoes and matching stockings.

1. Make a jumper, high waisted and flaring, to wear over a knitted sweater. Or with inset knit collar and sleeves.

2. Pick supple fabrics for a soft body-shaped dress with contrasting top and belt.

3. Team a long, high-waisted midi dress in plain fabric with contrasting embroidered or velvet appliquéd jacket.

4. Choose a plain style for a slightly flared tube dress in strong geometric fabric. Add features like contrasting suede tab opening and cuffs.

Creative hint: You can make No. 4 from our Basic Dress pattern. Place the center front on the fold of the fabric and make a seam and zipper opening along the center back. Cut a contrasting tab and attach it along the neck and down the center front by sewing on buttons through the tab and dress.

5. If you have a small waist, define it with a tight bodice, wide belt, pleated skirt. Once again, add strips of contrasting leather, suede or braid on bodice, sleeves, belt and scarf.

Daisy alphabet

Next time you want to put initials on your favorite scarf or hanky, do it with flowers. These initials are worked completely in lazy daisy stitch. To embroider letters the same size as those illustrated on a very fine linen or cotton, or a gauzy type of fabric, first trace the initials you want onto the fabric. Either draw in the whole daisy lightly with a very sharp yellow or white pencil, or simply put dots at the center and tips of the petals. Embroider the daisies with one strand of 6-strand floss or any fine embroidery thread.

If you want the back to look as good as the front, finish off each daisy separately. This gives a series of stars at the back of the embroidery. For a bold, gay look to decorate a pillow or a pocket on jeans or a dress, work the initials on a much larger scale with tapestry or crewel yarn. When working on a larger scale, make a center with a French knot.

The rest of the alphabet follows in the next Pattern Library chapter, page 221.

Pattern Library

Finishing, blocking and pressing

The finishing of a garment is very important. If you have followed the directions and made each piece with great care, it would be a pity to spoil all your work by being in too much of a hurry to give proper attention to the finishing.

Always check whether or not the directions tell you to press the pieces before you begin to finish them. It will be too late to realize that you must not press after you have already done so and certain man-made fibers can be completely ruined by contact with heat. So read first and be safe!

Blocking

If pressing is required, prepare the pieces by running in any yarn ends. To do this, darn the ends up the edges of the work which are to be seamed so that the ends are secure and cannot eventually work themselves loose.

Next, place each piece of knitting, right side down, on an ironing pad and pin evenly around the edges. If in doubt, always use too many pins rather than too few. Also, they should be the stainless steel variety, like tailor's pins, that won't leave rust marks. Never stretch the knitting or the pins will make a fluted edge. The shape you obtain when pinning should be the perfect finished shape which you seam. When the pieces are pinned, check with a ruler that the width and length are the same as those in the directions.

Pressing

Since an ironing board is too narrow for most knitted pieces, the knitter who wants a perfectly finished garment would be well advised to make herself an ironing pad. This can be done easily. First decide on the size and shape you want: It should be large enough to take a dress length and may be either square or oblong. To back the ironing pad use a piece of felt or wool, lay three or four pieces of blanket on top (old blanket pieces are ideal), then two layers of white sheet material. Bind all the edges together with wide bias tape. You now have a pressing pad which can be used on an unpolished hard surface like a kitchen table or even on the floor.

Rinse a clean, white, cotton cloth or piece of an old sheet in warm water, wring it out, and place it over the knitted work to be pressed. Do not allow the damp cloth to extend over any of the ribbed edges: These do not require pressing. With a warm iron, press the surface of the knitting evenly but not too heavily. You could spoil your work by pressing too hard, either by flattening the stitches beyond recognition or by leaving tell-tale iron marks. The iron should be pressed down and lifted up again, not moved along the surface as it would be in actual ironing. If you do use the ordinary ironing method, you will stretch and crease the

knitting, and thus spoil the perfect shape you have obtained by pinning the garment so carefully when you started. If any garter stitch or ribbing becomes pressed in error, it can be steamed back into shape (this applies only to wool and not to man-made fibers). But do, of course, be very careful not to direct the steam onto yourself as you hold the knitting in the jet of steam from a boiling kettle! The damp heat will soon make the over-flattened strands spring back into shape again.

Of course, this can become a tedious job if the area to be revived is very large. In this case, lay the piece to be treated on your ironing pad. Do not pin, simply pat it flat. Rinse and wring out your cloth in warm water again, place it flat over the knitting and leave until the ribbing, garter stitch or pattern springs back into life.

Knitting pinned in place for pressing with warm iron through damp cloth

Seams

To sew knitting, use a blunt-pointed needle as it is less likely to split the stitches and spoil the effect of a neat seam.

If the garment has been made in a fairly thick yarn, it is best to split the yarn for sewing or buy a thinner one in the same shade: Your work will be far easier and your result neater.

Backstitch seam

The backstitch seam is worked in very much the same way as in dressmaking except that it is important to keep looking at the other side of the seam to check that you are not splitting any of the stitches and are working along a straight line. Whether you work half or one stitch in from the edge is a matter of personal choice and may be determined by the thickness of the garment which is to be seamed.

Start sewing by working two small stitches, one on top of the other. *Now, with the needle at the back of the work, move along to the left, bringing the needle through to the front of the work the width of one stitch away from the last stitch. Take the needle back to the left-hand end of the last stitch and take it through to the back of the work. Repeat from * until the seam is complete. Care must be taken to pull the stitches firmly through the knitting so that they do not show an untidy line on the right side when finished. Do not stretch the seam by pulling it over your fingers, or draw it too tightly so that it becomes a different length from the knitting around it.

Backstitch seaming

Invisible seam

The photograph below shows the seam being worked on the right side of the work.

Begin by securing the sewing yarn to one side. Pass the needle directly across to the other side of the work, picking up one loop. Pass the needle directly back to the first side of the work, picking up one loop. Continue working in this way as if you were making rungs of a ladder but pull the stitches tight so that they are not seen on the right side when finished.

All seams should be pressed on the wrong side after completion.

Invisible seaming

Flat seam

This is the best seam to use when two edges are to be drawn together as in ribbing.

This method can also be worked on the wrong side working through the extreme edge stitches as seen in the diagram on the right. Pass the threaded darning needle through the edge stitch on the right-hand side directly across to the edge stitch on the left-hand side and pull the yarn through. Turn the needle and work through the next stitch on the left-hand side directly across to the edge stitch on the right-hand side, again pulling the yarn through. Continue up the seam in this manner.

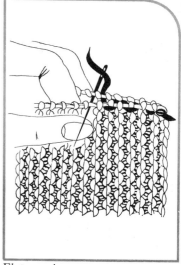

Flat seaming

Sewing in a pocket

Pockets

When sewing either patch or inserted pockets, they must be absolutely in line with the knitted stitches and rows. The best way is to run a fine knitting needle up the line of the stitches to be followed, picking up alternate loops; the edge is slip stitched to these loops. It is very important that the cast-on lower edge lies straight along a row.

Casing stitch

Casing stitch is often referred to in making-up instructions where a waist edge requires a non-bulky hem to carry elastic, as on a skirt. The strongest and most satisfactory method of working is to crochet a zig- zag chain using the same yarn as used for the garment. The number of chains used to form the sloping sides of the zigzag will depend on the width of the elastic which you plan to use for a particular garment.

Casing stitch

The drummer boy coat

Basic Wardrobe Knitting

These delightful little coats with their fresh, simple lines are worked in a firm fabric stitch. The double-breasted front fastening is worked separately and can be adapted for either a boy or a girl. Contrast piping is made by working the invisible casting on method. Shoulder tabs and a back half-belt give a crisp, military air.

Sizes

Directions are for 20in chest. Length down center back, 16¼ [17¾:19¼]in.
Sleeve seam, 6½ [8½:10½]in. The figures in brackets [ ] refer to the 22 and 24in sizes respectively.

> **Basic gauge**
> 6sts and 7 rows to 1 inch measured over stockinette stitch worked on No.5 needles.
> **Gauge for this design**
> 7½sts and 13 rows on No.4 needles.

Materials

Reynolds Classique 50 gr balls
5 [6:7] balls in main color, A
2 balls in contrast, B
One pair No. 3 needles or Canadian No. 10
One pair No. 4 needles or Canadian No. 9
Two stitch holders
Ten medium buttons
Two small buttons
Small quantity of Sports yarn in any color for casting on. This is removed afterwards.

Note

If the coat is being made for a girl, complete the left front first and mark the button positions on this side. The buttonholes are then worked on the right side. If making the coat for a boy, complete the right front first and work the buttonholes on the left front.

Back

Using No.3 needles and a length of odd wool, cast on 61 [67:73] sts. (This thread is removed later.)
** **Next row** With B, K1, *ytf, K1, rep from * to end. 121 [133:145] sts.
Next row K1, * ytf, sl1, ytb, K1, rep from * to end.
Next row Ytf, sl1, ytb, * K1, ytf, sl1, ytb, rep from * to end.
Rep last 2 rows once more. Break B and remove thread used for casting on.**
Using A and No.4 needles, begin pattern:
1st row Sl1, K to end.
2nd row Sl1, K to end.
3rd row P1, * ytb, sl1, ytf, P1, rep from * to end.
4th row K1, * ytf, sl1, ytb, K1, rep from * to end.
These 4 rows form the pattern and are rep throughout.
Work 16 rows more.
1st dec row K29 [32:35], sl1, K1, psso, K2 tog, K55 [61:67], sl1, K1, psso, K2 tog, K29 [32:35].
Keeping pattern correct, work 15 rows more.
2nd dec row K28 [31:34], sl1, K1, psso, K2 tog, K53 [59:65], sl1, K1, psso, K2 tog, K28 [31:34].
Work 15 rows more.
Continue dec 4sts in this way on next and every 16th row until 89 [97:105] sts rem.
Work until 11 [12¼:13½]in,

ending with a WS row.

Shape armholes

Bind off 4 [5:6] sts at beg of next 2 rows.
Dec one st at each end of next 6 rows, then next 0 [1:2] RS rows.
Work 46[47:47] rows more.

Shape shoulders

Bind off at each armhole edge 5sts 0 [2:4] times and 4sts 10 [8:6] times.
Bind off rem sts.

Left front

Using No.3 needles and a length of odd wool, cast on 37 [41:45] sts.
Work from ** to ** as for Back.
Next row With A, knit to last 22 [24:26] sts and leave these sts on holder for front panel.
Continue on No.4 needles with A in pattern as given for back, beginning with 2nd pattern row. Work 19 rows.
1st dec row K29 [32:35], sl1, K1, psso, K2 tog, K18 [21:24].
Work 15 rows more.
2nd dec row K28 [31:34], sl1, K1, psso, K2 tog, K17 [20:23].
Work 15 rows more.
Continue dec 2sts on next and every 16th row until 35 [39:43] sts rem.
Work until same length as back to armhole, ending at side edge.

Shape armhole

1st row Bind off 4 [5:6] sts, pattern to end.
Work one row.
Dec at armhole edge on next 6 rows, then next 0 [1:2] RS rows.
Work 29 rows more without shaping.

Shape neck

Dec one st at center front on next and every other row until 20 [21:22] sts rem.
Work until same length as back to shoulder, ending at the armhole edge.

Shape shoulder

Bind off 5sts every other row 0 [1:2] times and 4sts every other row 5 [4:3] times.

Right front

Cast on and work from ** to ** as for left front.
Next row With B and still using No.3 needles, K22 [24:26].
Slip these sts onto holder until required.
Continue in pattern with A and No.4 needles.
Work 20 rows.
1st dec row K18 [21:24], sl1, K1, psso, K2 tog, K29 [32:35].
Work 15 rows more.
2nd dec row K17 [20:23], sl1, K1, psso, K2 tog, K28 [31:34].
Work 15 rows more.
Continue as for left front, reversing all shapings.

Button strip

Slip 22 [24:26] sts from holder onto No.3 needles.
With B and RS work facing, K across sts from holder.
Continue in garter st (every row K) until strip is long enough to reach beg of neck shaping when slightly stretched.
Bind off.
Mark positions for four groups of buttons.
Work strip on other side in same way, working buttonholes when markers are reached as follows:
RS work facing, K3, bind off 3, K to last 6sts, bind off 3, K3.
Next row K3, cast on 3, K to last 3sts, cast on 3, K3.

Sleeves

Using No.3 needles and a length of odd wool, cast on 25 [27:29] sts.
Work as for back from ** to ** 49 [53:57] sts.
Continue on No.4 needles with A in 4 row pattern as for back.
Work 4 [4:12] rows.
Keeping pattern correct, inc one st at each end of next and every 8th [8th:12th] row until there are 69 [73:77] sts.
Work until sleeve measures 6½ [8½:10½]in or required length.

Shape cap

Bind off 4 [5:6] sts at beg of

next 2 rows.
Dec one st at each end of every
RS row until 33sts rem.
Dec one st at each end of next
7 rows.
Bind off.

Neckband

Sew shoulder seams and sl st
button and buttonhole strips
to their respective sides.
Beginning 1 inch before seam of
front strip to main front, and
using No.4 needles, K7 sts
from right front strip, K13
[14:15] sts up right front
neck to shoulder, K21
[23:25] sts from back, K13
[14:15] sts down left front
neck and K7 sts from left
front strip, finishing about 1
inch beyond front strip seam
to main section.
K one row.
Beginning with a 3rd pattern
row, work 6 rows in 4 row
pattern as for back. Break A.
Change to No.3 needles and B.
1st row K1, * ytf, sl1, ytb,
K1, rep from * to end.
2nd row Ytf, sl1, ytb,
* K1, ytf, sl1, ytb, rep
from * to end.
Rep 1st and 2nd rows once.
Break B, leaving a length of
yarn for working the invisible
binding off.
Bind off using a darning
needle as shown in chapter 4.

Belt

With No.3 needles and B, cast
on 11sts.
K 42 [48:54] rows. Bind off.

Shoulder tabs

With No.3 needles and B, cast
on 9sts.
K 20 [22: 24] rows.

Shape point
1st row K1, sl1, K1, psso,
K to last 3sts, K2 tog, K1,
K one row.
Rep last 2 rows once.
5th row K1, sl1, K2 tog,
psso, K1.
6th row Sl1, K2 tog, psso,
pull yarn through and
finish off.
Work another tab in the
same way.

▲ *Back view of the coats*

Finishing

Press very lightly under a damp
cloth with a warm iron.
Join side and sleeve seams.
Sew in sleeves.
Fold edge of neckband
sideways and sl st to bound-
off edge of front strips.
Sew belt to center back and
sew a button at either end.
Stitch cast-on edge of tabs
close to sleeve seam at shoulder.
Sew point in place toward
neckband and trim with a
small button.
Sew buttons to correspond
with buttonholes.
Press seams lightly.

Little drummer boy ►

▼ *Detail of invisible casting on*

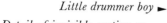

Crochet Know-how 11

Rainbows & Wagon Wheels

Crochet looks especially gay and charming when it is worked in rounds. Of course, the character of various designs differs enormously, depending on whether you use a rainbow of colors, as in the pillows below, or different tones of a single color, as in the wagon wheel afghan in the photograph opposite. Buying the actual yarn to match a color scheme you imagine can be difficult, it's true. If you want help, there is a beautiful kaleidoscopic color wheel and notes on combining shades in Embroidery chapter 5, page 88.

Wagon wheels

To make the large round
Ch4. Join into circle with ss.
1st round. Ch3, * (yoh, insert hook into the circle and draw a loop through) twice, yoh and draw through all loops, ch1, rep from * 7 more times. Join with ss into 3rd ch. Cut yarn and fasten off.
2nd round. Join new color into last ch sp with a ss, ch2, (1dc, ch2) into same sp,* (2dc, ch2) into next ch sp, rep from * 6 times (8 dc groups). Join with a ss into 2nd ch. Cut yarn and fasten off.
3rd round. Join new color into last ch sp with a ss, ch2, (1dc, ch1, 2dc, ch1) into same sp,* (2dc, ch1, 2dc, ch1) into next ch sp, rep from * to end (16 dc groups). Join as before. Cut yarn and fasten off.
4th round. Join new color into last sp with ss, ch2, (2dc, ch1) into same sp,* (3dc, ch1) into next ch sp, rep from * to end (16 dc groups). Cut yarn and fasten off.
5th round. Change color and rep 4th round once more.

To make the small round
Make a ch and work 1st round as above but do not break yarn.
2nd round. Ch2, (1dc, ch2) into next sp,* (2dc, ch2) into each sp to end. Join with ss. Cut yarn and fasten off.

Rainbows for a round pillow cover

This is worked on the same principle as the wagon wheel.
Ch4. Join into circle with ss.
Rounds 1-4. Work as for the large wagon wheel.
5th round. Join new color into last sp with a ss, ch2, (2tr, ch2) into same sp,* (3tr, ch2) into next ch sp, rep from * to end. Cut yarn and fasten off.
6th round. Join new color into last sp with a ss, ch3, (3tr, ch2) into same sp,* (4tr, ch2) into next sp, rep from * to end. Cut yarn and fasten off.
7th round. Join new color into last sp with ss, ch3, (4tr, ch2) into same sp,* (5tr, ch2) into next sp, rep from * to end. Cut yarn and fasten off.
Work next 3 rounds in same way as 7th round, working 1 extra

tr in each group in succeeding rounds.
11th round. Join new color into last ch sp with ss, ch2 (1dc, ch1) into same sp, * skip 2dc, (2dc, ch1) into next dc, skip 3dc, (2dc, ch1) into next dc, (2dc, ch1) into next sp, rep from * to end. Cut yarn and fasten off.
12th round. Join new color into last sp with ss, ch2, 2dc into same sp, * 3dc into next sp, rep from * to end.
Work 4 rounds more as 12th round, working ch1 between dc groups. Work second side in the same way. Sew rounds together, leaving an opening to insert the pillow.

The patchwork pillow cover

Both this square pillow cover and the one below begin with the American Granny square already used for the afghan in Crochet chapter 5.
Make a square arranging your choice of colors as in the illustration, working eight rounds.
9th round. Work 3dc into each sp omitting the ch1 between groups, except at the corners which are worked as before.
10th round. Work 1dc into each dc in the previous row, working corners as before.
Sew the squares together on the wrong side, or crochet using sc. Make tassels and attach to corners.

The square pillow cover

Make one square arranging your choice of colors as in the illustration, working seven rounds. Work the 8th round as for the 9th round in the patchwork cushion.
Continue working in dc groups as before, working into every 3rd dc for next round. Continue until 15 rounds in all have been worked.
Next round. Work alternate groups of 3tr and 2tr separated by ch1 along sides, working 2 groups of 3tr with ch1 between into corners.
Work next round in the same way.
Last 2 rounds. Work sc into each st of previous row.
Edging. Work picot edging by working * 1sc into each of next 2 sts, ch3, rep from * around all edges.

▼ *Multi-colored pillow covers*   *Wagon wheel afghan* ►

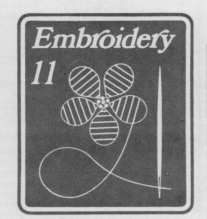

Embroidery 11

A flourish of ferns

In this chapter you will find four more beautiful fern designs. These complete the set of eight which was specially designed for Creative Hands. The other ferns appear in Embroidery chapter 6, page 108 and chapter 9, page 168.

As before, the charts all include detailed stitch references. There are also instructions for five attractive new stitches used in the fern embroideries, in addition to the ones already given in earlier chapters.

Trace and transfer the fern designs from the line drawing to your fabric (see directions given in Embroidery chapter 4, page 68). You can if you wish, enlarge the designs at this stage and you will find full details of this technique in Embroidery chapter 15, page 286. The color scheme chosen by the designer is by no means the only possibility, and you may well prefer to choose your own. The actual texture of the many lovely stitches will take on added importance if you work them all in one color. White on a dark background, perhaps navy or scarlet, would be particularly effective, or, again dark threads on a light background. Black and white is always an extremely flattering combination, whether you choose to embroider a black design on a white background or the other way around.

For a more sumptuous effect, perhaps for a caftan or an evening skirt with a matching stole, work the ferns in silver or gold threads on a rich purple textured silk.

Suggestions for using the fern designs

The original fern designs were worked with a single fern on each of six elegant place mats, with the Scolopendrium officinarum and the Platycerium alcicorne designs at each end of a table runner. There are, however, many other exciting ways to apply the designs. Here are some of them.

In the kitchen and dining room—on a wall hanging, apron or tablecloth; in the living room—on a table runner, pillows, or book covers, and as pictures with small gold frames, or as one large botanical print framed in silver or maple wood; in the bedroom—on a pajama case, headboard panel or as a frieze along a pair of curtains; in the bathroom—a single fern on a guest towel.

Ferns as place mats

The quickest and easiest way is to embroider the ferns onto a set of ready-made mats, but if you are expert enough to make your own, here is what you will need: For six place mats each 12in by 18in and a large center mat 12in by 36in, you will need 1¼ yds of 54in wide linen. The ferns shown here are worked on natural, but there is a wide range of colors in dress-weight linen to choose from and each fern can look quite different when worked on another color background. Use two strands of 6-strand embroidery floss either in similar shades to those chosen by the designer or a color combination of your own choice.

1. Woven spider web
Work straight stitches from the center of the circle, building up an uneven number of foundation threads. Then, working from the center, weave over one stitch, under one stitch until the circle is filled.

2. Ribbed or backstitched spider web
The base is formed by working two cross-stitches to form an eight-spoked star. Then cover with a continuous line of backstitch starting from the center.

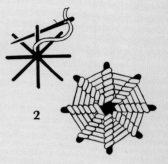

3. Double knot stitch
Make a small diagonal stitch over the line of design, bring the needle back and slip it under the thread once, then again under the same thread, making a buttonhole loop stitch. When this stitch is worked closely together it gives an attractive bold line.

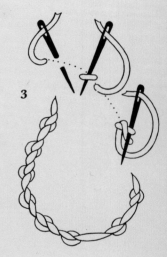

4. Surface darning
First make a foundation of closely worked satin stitch. Then, with either a matching or contrasting thread, weave over and under the foundation threads only and not through the fabric, except at the beginning and end of each row. If the foundation threads are slightly spaced, an open effect results.

5. Butterfly chain stitch
First work a row of vertical straight stitches in groups of three, then bunch each group of stitches together with a chain stitch to make a butterfly. The chain stitch is not worked through the fabric.

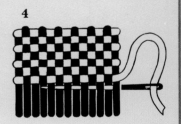

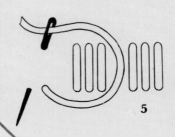

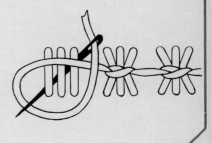

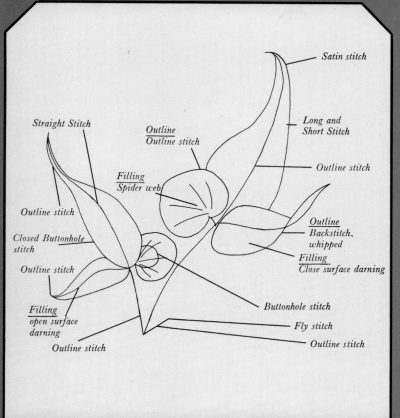

Straight Stitch

Outline
Outline stitch

Filling
Spider web

Satin stitch

Long and
Short Stitch

Outline stitch

Outline
Backstitch,
whipped

Filling
Close surface darning

Outline stitch

Closed Buttonhole
stitch

Outline stitch

Filling
open surface
darning

Outline stitch

Buttonhole stitch

Fly stitch

Outline stitch

Design chart showing stitches for Andiantum Wilsoni (above) and Doryopteris Pedata (below)

Here you see the final embroidered versions of the ferns, worked in the colors chosen by the designer

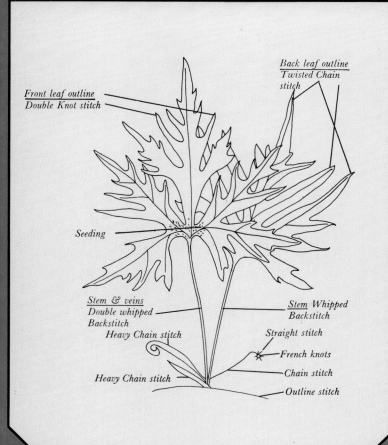

Back leaf outline
Twisted Chain
stitch

Front leaf outline
Double Knot stitch

Seeding

Stem & veins
Double whipped
Backstitch
Heavy Chain stitch

Heavy Chain stitch

Stem Whipped
Backstitch

Straight stitch

French knots

Chain stitch

Outline stitch

Ferns as pictures

On this page you'll see how decorative the ferns look mounted in gold frames. The names of these particular ferns are Platycerium Alcicorne and Woodwardia Areolata. If you prefer to plan a picture on a larger scale, work all eight designs on one large piece of fabric. Back firmly with woven interfacing and sew onto chunky bamboo rods to make an impressive botanical wall hanging.

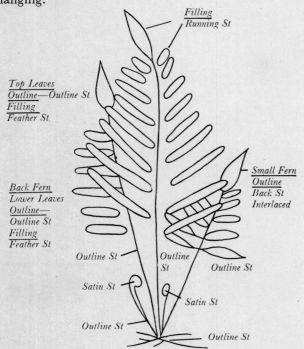

Filling
Running St

Top Leaves
Outline—Outline St
Filling
Feather St

Small Fern
Outline
Back St
Interlaced

Back Fern
Lower Leaves
Outline—
Outline St
Filling
Feather St

Outline St

Outline St

Outline St

Satin St

Satin St

Outline St

Outline St

In design form: ▲ *Woodwardia Areolata* ▼ *Platycerium Alcicorne*

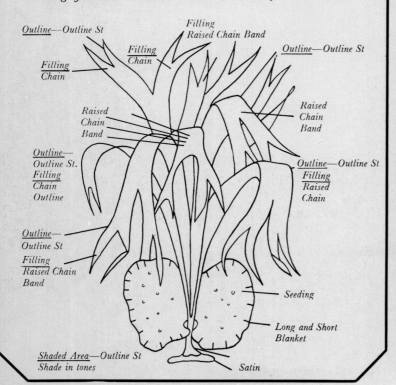

Outline—Outline St

Filling
Raised Chain Band

Filling
Chain

Outline—Outline St

Filling
Chain

Raised
Chain
Band

Raised
Chain
Band

Outline—
Outline St.
Filling
Chain
Outline

Outline—Outline St
Filling
Raised
Chain

Outline—
Outline St
Filling
Raised Chain
Band

Seeding

Long and Short
Blanket

Shaded Area—Outline St
Shade in tones

Satin

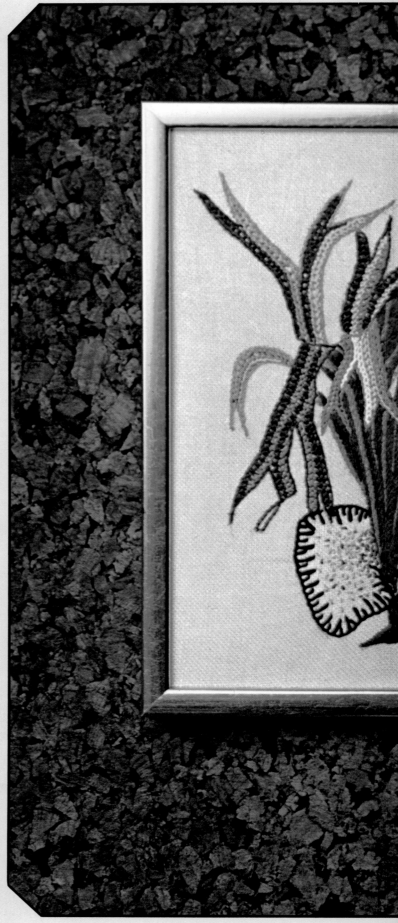

210

Make a belt with Cross-stitch

Despite its simplicity, cross-stitch can be extremely effective and adaptable. These patterns, for example, make marvelous belts and borders. It is fascinating to experiment with color schemes, because a design originally in one color combination will look entirely different in another.

Materials

To obtain a design about $\frac{2}{3}$ of the size of the motifs illustrated on the opposite page, use double-thread canvas with 14 threads to the inch and tapestry yarn, 6-strand floss or a soft embroidery cotton. You can adapt designs to coarser or finer canvas, using appropriately thicker or finer yarns.

Cross-stitch

To work cross-stitch make a row of slanting stitches from left to right and then make another row from right to left on top of them. The picture below shows the stitch worked with a thin yarn so that you can see clearly how it builds up. When it is worked correctly, the canvas should be completely covered with yarn. Each cross-stitch should add up to a perfect square and must always be worked over an equal number of threads, down and across. The main point to remember is that the upper stitches must always lie in the same direction.

Method of working cross-stitch

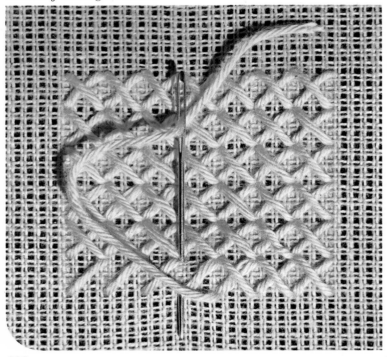

A selection of design and gift ideas using cross-stitch

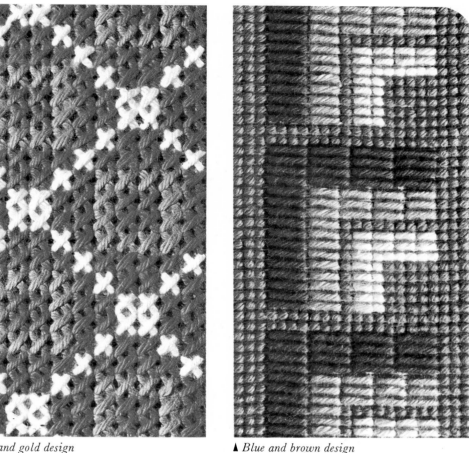

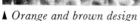

▲ *Orange and brown design*

▲ *Red and gold design*

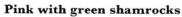

▲ *Blue and brown design*

Orange and brown design

This is a simple pattern using square motifs in three colors. Try using three tones of one color or, for a checkerboard effect, use a black background with gray and white centers. For an all-over design, the square motifs could be grouped to form geometric patterns. With an interesting use of color against a contrasting background shade, a fascinating patchwork effect can be achieved.

Red and gold design

This motif lends itself to being repeated over a large area and readily adapts for a cummerbund, bag, stool top, pillow cover or chair seat. Or make an exotic vest in gold, copper and silver metallic yarns.

Blue and brown design

This L-shaped repeat motif is stitched in upright Gobelin stitch (see Needlepoint chapter 4, page 92) worked over 4, 3 and 2 double threads of canvas. The background is worked over 1 thread. A three-dimensional effect is obtained by using tones of one color for the L-shape. This motif can be adapted to build up geometric designs.

Pink with green shamrocks

Use half cross-stitch or tent stitch for this pretty design. If you make this up in a different combination of colors, the whole character of the design becomes more sophisticated. To add more texture, you could work the background or the shamrocks in tiny cross-stitch, or tram the shamrocks to give a raised effect.

Pink with green shamrocks ▼

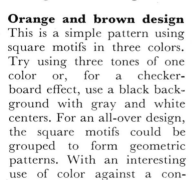

Daisy joining

Once you have learned to make daisies with closed centers (Daisy work chapter 1, page 194), you can begin to be more ambitious. In this chapter you will discover how to work daisies with open centers and decorate them with beads. The edges of the daisies lend themselves to decoration, too. The lock stitch edging explained here makes for a neat, stylized finish which holds the petals firmly in their original shape. If you want to make your daisies into a trimming, this edging is part of the basic method. You'll find that square daisies (using the Knit-Wit) are easy, too—if you want to prove it to yourself, make the adorable crib blanket opposite.

Open centers

Thread needle with end of yarn. Put needle into center of daisy and pull it through between any two petals. Put needle into center again and bring it out between the next two petals, working clockwise. Continue overcasting, working an extra (13th) stitch to make the center complete. Finish off by threading the needle through the loop of the 13th stitch before pulling it tight. Then thread the needle under the overcasting to hide the knot.

Decorative centers

There's no end to the ways you can decorate daisies. Add a pearl or rhinestone to the center for evening daisies or colored wooden or glass beads, buttons (the smooth, rounded ones which have a shank at the back for sewing to the fabric) or even sunflower seeds. When you finish overcasting, push the needle up through the center, thread it through the pearl or rhinestone, then sew through the opposite side of the hole. Make another overcasting stitch there to secure the bead, then draw the needle through the loop of the next stitch and finish off as for the open center daisy.

214

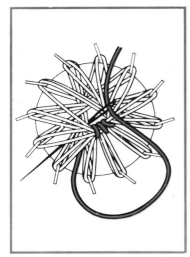

Overcasting an open center

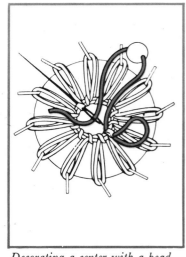

Decorating a center with a bead

Lock stitch edging

1. Make a daisy in the usual way but leave an end 14 inches long when you begin. Then, keeping the daisy on the daisy maker, thread up with the end of yarn. Take the needle upward through the center of a petal to the left of the spoke. Thread the needle through again, to the right of the spoke, leaving the loop.

2. Thread the needle through this loop from right to left and pull tight with a gentle jerk so that the knot locks below the spoke. Stitch each petal in turn in the same way, leaving a fairly loose thread between each spoke. When circle is complete, take end of yarn back to the center and finish off. Release the daisy from the daisy maker.

To join round daisies

Make one daisy complete with lock stitch edging. Make a second, without the edging, and leave it on the daisy maker. Taking the completed daisy, place it wrong side up to cover the daisy on the daisy maker. Begin the lock stitch edging, going through two petals only of both top and bottom daisy.

Turn back the top daisy and finish edging the bottom daisy as described in **2.**

When making a chain of more than two daisies for a pretty trim or dress edge, be sure to join the petals directly opposite the previous joining.

Square daisies

Place the adapter on the Knit-Wit and wind yarn across it from spoke to spoke, following the directions for the round daisy. The yarn will lie across the opening of each post. Make two windings, overcast stitches in the center, and lock stitch edging according to the directions for the round daisy. Join square daisies as round ones, except join 4 petals of top square to 4 of bottom one. Start at one post of adapter, working the following 2 spokes, and finishing the joining at the 2nd post of the adapter (1 complete side of square).

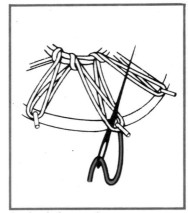

Lock stitch: step **1**

Lock stitch: step **2**

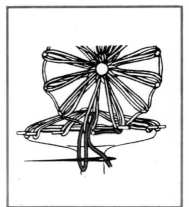

Joining two daisies

Square daisy on adapter

Daisy babies

Making a crib blanket is a perfect way to start joining square daisies. It's small enough for individual daisies to retain their importance, is quick to finish and lends itself to pretty decoration. Here the centers of some of the daisies have been embroidered to emphasize their 'daisy-ness', but you could apply a few separate daisies instead, or attach a pompon to each corner, or make each in a different color for a patchwork effect.

You will need: 6oz Bernat Berella Baby Bulky yarn and 1oz of contrast yarn (100% orlon for washability). Knit-Wit.

The blanket consists of eleven rows of fifteen square daisies. Follow the instructions for making and joining these on the previous page. When the first row is completed, add each new individual daisy by working lock stitch edging to form the next row and by joining each addition to the previous row as well as to one another. Oversew the centers of the daisies around the edge with contrast yarn and also decorate a ring of centers down the middle.

The basic dress continued

In this chapter the pieces are assembled and the finishing touches are put to the dress.

Step 1

Front fastening, tab (continued). Before you stitch the tab to the dress, prepare the corner on the dress front as shown in the diagram below, to prevent it from fraying.

Machine stitch a row of stay stitches just outside the marked-out stitching line, then cut into the corner without cutting the stay stitches.

Pin, baste and stitch the raw edge of the tab to the right dress front on the tab stitching line, but avoid catching the facing fabric into the seam. Spread the corner on the dress so that you can stitch comfortably toward the pointed end of the tab. Make sure that the corner stays in position and does not drag inward, by pivoting the machine needle just inside the stay stitching at the corner. The point of the tab must be in line with the

center front seam.

If the fabric is thick and the seam allowance on the tab at the corner does not lie flat after pressing, trim it carefully across the corner.

Fold under the seam allowance on the facing and pin it over the seamline to cover the raw edges. Slip stitch in place by hand. Remove all remaining basting on the tab.

To press the tab, lay it full length, wrong side up, on the ironing board with the sides of the dress front fully supported. Fold the left front double to keep it out of the way of the iron, but without dragging the center front seam, and press.

The wrap. To complete the center front fastening, make the wrap on the left front edge. Cut out the facing from the lining fabric, leaving a $\frac{3}{4}$in seam allowance, using the tab pattern as your guide, but without the pointed end. Instead, extend both sides of the

tab pattern to the length of the point and cut straight across the lower edge, not forgetting the seam allowance. It is not necessary to mark the seam-line of the facing strip, as you can use the marking on the dress front for your stitching lines.

Pin and baste the facing to the left front edge of the dress, with right sides facing. Stitch the facing and fabric together, starting at the center front, along the top edge and down the front, leaving the lower edge unstitched.

Trim the seam allowance, clip into the seam at the beginning of the stitching line (center front), and turn the facing into the dress. Baste firmly along the sewed edges and press carefully.

Turn under the long raw edge on the facing until it is even with the meeting line for the tab, and sew it with a slip stitch. Working on the inside, lay the wrap over the tab and you will see that the center front seam folds over too. To make the seam lie flat and open, cut into the seam allowance as shown below, press the seam

open and press the wrap over the tab.

Oversew the raw lower edge of the wrap facing by hand, catching in the center front seam allowance.

To hold the wrap in position, make several small stitches at the lower edge, catching it to the stitching line of the tab.

The fastening detail is now complete, so give it a final pressing.

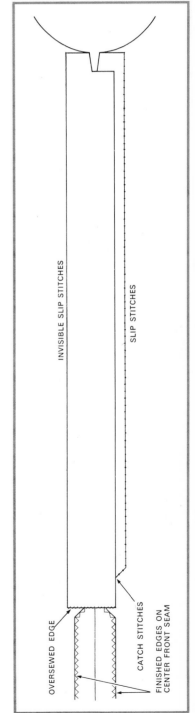

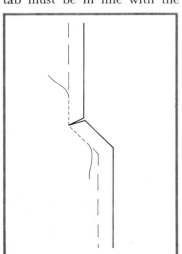

The stay-stitched corner

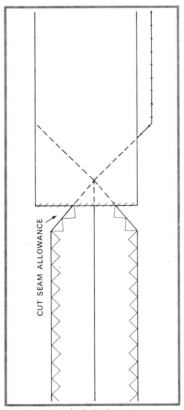

Detail of the stitched wrap

Finished stitched wrap inside

Step 2

The dress back: Darts. First stitch the darts at the shoulder if you are using them.

Slash the darts along the center to within 1½in from the point and press them open as for a seam. This way they will lie flat when the shoulder seam is stitched and not leave a bump showing above the seam. Overcast the raw edges to finish them off.

If you are darting the waist, stitch the darts and then press them toward the center.

Step 3

Joining the dress sections: Shoulder seams. Pin, baste and stitch the shoulder seams, matching balance marks and seamlines. Overcast the raw seam edges. Remove the basting. Press seams open.

Side seams. Working on a flat surface, lay the side seams together. Match the side seam balance marks on the back to the ends of the side bust darts on the front. Pin, baste and stitch the side seams, making sure that both layers of fabric are perfectly smooth, otherwise the side seams will not hang straight.

Overcast the raw seam edges and remove the basting. Press the seams open. Take out any impressions the seam may have made on the fabric by running your iron under the seam allowance.

Overcasting the seam edges

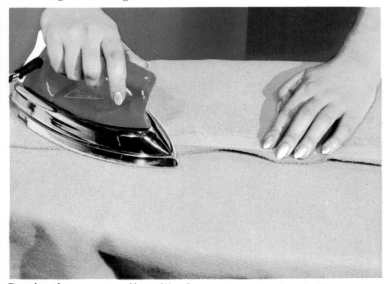

Pressing the seam open. You will, of course, use a pressing cloth!

Step 4

Finishing the dress. When you make a garment with sleeves, it is important to finish the neckline first, as it is essential to see if the firm fit of the collar affects the armhole line over the shoulders. When you make a sleeveless dress, it does not matter if you finish the armhole edge first.

The armhole edge is finished here so that you can see the technique more clearly.

The armholes. First measure the size of the armholes along the seamline.

Find the true bias of the facing fabric by laying one side of a 45° set square to the selvage of the fabric, and mark the diagonal of the fabric with pins or tailor's chalk (see layout of facing fabric in the Pattern Pack).

Cut 1½in wide bias strips of facing fabric and join them as shown on the diagram to make up the length required for the armholes plus 2in for ease and 1in for seam allowance.

The bias strips will have to be curved to follow the line of the armholes. To do this, place one bias strip on the ironing board and press around the outer edge, gently stretching this into a curve as you press; then press in the fullness along the inner edge of the curve so that the material is as flat as possible.

Turn under ½in seam allowance at one end of the bias strip.

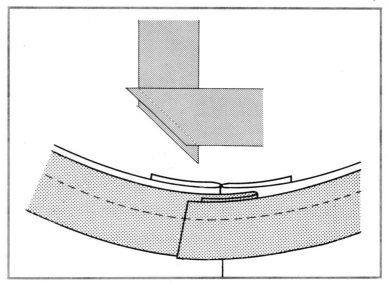

Top: Joining bias strips   Bottom: Bias strip basted around lower armhole

Starting at this end and working on the outside of the dress with right sides facing, pin the inner curved edge of the bias strip around the armhole seamline. Start at the top of the side seam and take only $\frac{3}{16}$in seam allowance. The inner curve on the bias will still be a little full and you will have to ease the fullness into the underarm curve of the armhole seam.

Let the end of the bias overlap the turned-under seam allowance, as this will make for a secure joining and also give a little extra stretch where you need it.

Because the curve of the armhole shape varies so much, it is not advisable to join the ends of the bias strip in the straight of the grain where they meet at the side seam, as is usual with a straight edge. So leave the strip untrimmed and unstitched until the facing is complete, then stitch it as it falls.

Leaving the overlap still unstitched, baste the bias firmly in position and machine stitch it in place around the armhole seamline.

Remove the basting stitches and trim the armhole seam allowance on the dress to the width of the seam allowance on the bias.

Clip into the seam allowance on the dress only to within a grain or two of the stitches, then turn the bias to the inside. Roll the seam

Hand sewing the armhole facing in position

edge slightly to the inside to prevent the bias from showing, and baste in place. Press the basted edge gently. Turn the raw edge of the bias under for about ½in and pin and baste it to the dress. Now carefully hand sew the bias in place.

Slip stitch the lapped ends of the bias in place.

Remove all basting stitches and give one final pressing.

Face the other armhole in the same way.

The collar. The first consideration is whether you need to enlarge the collar. If you had to make the neckline larger, you will also need to cut a new collar pattern.

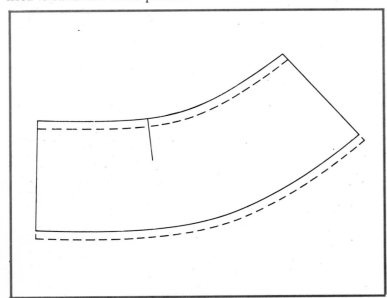

The dotted lines indicate where to enlarge the collar pattern

218

Measure the new stitching line around the neck edge of the dress. Halve this measurement and deduct ¼in.

To find this length on the collar pattern, measure into the collar from the neck edge and draw a new stitching line inside and parallel to the original neck stitching line of the pattern.

Mark the new position of the balance marks. Then cut the pattern along the new stitching line.

Place the cut pattern on a sheet of paper and pencil around it. Then add the amount you trimmed off the neck edge to the outer edge of the new collar pattern, so that the collar remains the same width as before.

Using the new pattern, cut the collar from the dress fabric. Remember to place the center back of the pattern on the fold of the fabric and to add and mark with tailor's tacks the ¾in seam allowance all around the outer edges.

Before you can put the collar together, you will need to cut out an under collar.

Fold the facing fabric in the position shown in the layout and cut out the under collar, allowing only ⅝in for seams. This will make

Pressing the collar

the under collar slightly smaller, and you will see why later.

Before removing the pattern, mark the balance marks. Remove pattern and mark the ordinary seam allowance ¾in on the neck edge of the under collar, but do not mark the seam allowance on the outer edge.

With the outer raw edges even, pin and baste the collar and under collar together around the outer, not neck, edge using the seam-line on the top collar as your guide.

Working with the under collar uppermost, stitch around the collar leaving the neck edge open.

Remove the basting thread, cut off the seam allowance across the corners and trim it along the stitched edges.

Now turn the collar to the right side and you will see why the under collar is cut slightly smaller than the collar; this is to prevent the under collar from showing on the outside.

Baste along the stitched edges, rolling the upper collar edge under so that both pieces lie perfectly flat. Press lightly.

With the right side of the outer collar facing the wrong side of the dress, pin, baste and stitch them together along the neck edge, with

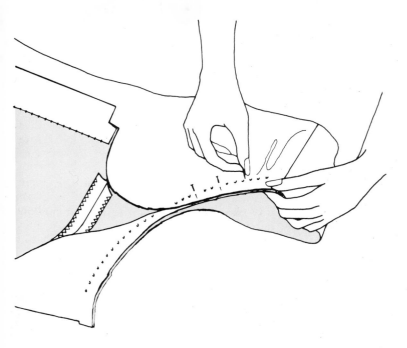

Pinning the collar to the dress

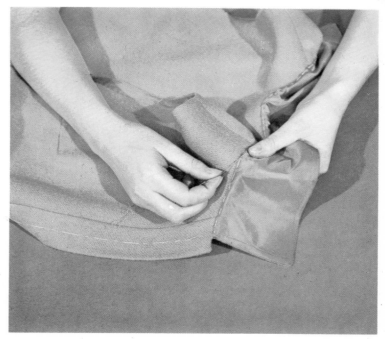

Slip stitching the collar facing

the ends of the collar meeting on the center front lines on the dress fronts.

Trim both seam allowances and snip into the allowance on the collar only. Press the seam into the collar.

Turn in the raw edge on the under collar for a full ¾in seam allowance and pin. To avoid strain at the center front you may have to adjust the depth of the seam allowance on your under collar. Snip into it as for the collar, then baste it to the stitching line so that the seam is just covered by the folded edge.

Slip stitch neatly in place.

Remove all basting and press.

The hem. After you have checked the hem, turn it up and finish it exactly as you did on the skirt in Dressmaking chapter 7, page 136.

Finishing the fastening. All that remains to be done is to sew on the snap fasteners and buttons.

To find the correct position for the snap fasteners it is necessary to work out the button positions first.

Use 8 buttons to trim the tab. Mark the place for the first button 1in down from the neck edge. Measure the remaining length of the tab and work out equal distances for 7 more buttons, leaving half a button distance between the last button and the pointed end of the tab. Mark the button positions along the center front line with pins so that you can see them on both sides of the tab. Sew on the snap fasteners first, one under each button position. Sew the ball part of the fastener to the tab and the sockets to the wrap. To find the socket positions on the center front line of the wrap, fold the tab over and mark the corresponding positions with pins.

To hold the top corner of the tab under the collar when it is fastened, sew on a snap fastener as shown in the picture.

Finally, sew one button over each of the other snap fasteners on the outside of the tab.

Give the dress one more careful pressing and it is ready to wear!

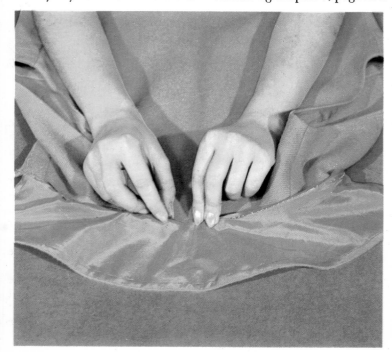

Turning under the lower edge of the collar facing

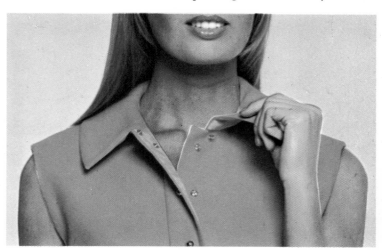

This shows the position of the snap fasteners

Fashion Flair

Capes, tunics and skirts

Here's a great fashion look that's easy to emulate. Tunics like the ones illustrated above can be made using the Creative Hands Pattern Pack. Simply adapt the pattern for either the shirtwaist dress or the shirt with tails. Team up capes with dresses, tunics with pants, and jackets with skirts.

Give a cape an interesting and luxurious look by lining it with a marvelous print or a quilted or fur fabric (1). Wear it over a long tunic or pants.

Vary the look by wearing a shorter tunic over pants of a deeper tone of the same color but with a different texture (2) or by making a high-collared tunic (4).

Adapt this look for evening wear

by making the tunic in rich, strongly patterned fabric (3). Velvet is ideal, and most large stores have a wide variety to choose from.

If you have a favorite jacket you cannot bear to throw away, revive it by teaming it with a new six-gore skirt. Co-ordinate them by facing the jacket lapels with skirt material (5) and finish off with tucked-in shirt and deep belt.